REBUILDING PRAIRIES AND FORESTS

Natalie Goldstein

Technical Consultants
Jerry J. Crockett, Ph.D., C.P.E.
Professor Emeritus of Ecology
Oklahoma State University

Jill Mahon
Forestry Consultant

CHILDRENS PRESS®
CHICAGO

A production of B&B Publishing, Inc.

Editor – Jean Black
Photo Editor – Margie Benson
Computer Specialist – Katy O'Shea

Interior Design – Jean Black/Dave Conant
Artist – Barbara Hammer

Library of Congress Cataloging-in-Publication Data

Goldstein, Natalie
    Rebuilding prairies and forests / by Natalie Goldstein.
       p. cm.
    Includes index.
    ISBN 0-516-05542-9
    1. Prairie conservation -- Juvenile literature. 2. Forest conservation --
Juvenile literature. 3. Prairie ecology -- Juvenile literature. 4. Forest ecology --
Juvenile literature. [1. Prairie conservation. 2. Forest conservation. 3. Prairie
ecology. 4. Ecology.] I. Title.
QH75.G62 1994
333.74'153--dc20
                                    94-18008
                                       CIP
                                       AC

Cover Photo: The Tallgrass Prairie Preserve in Oklahoma

Title Page: A Forest Service worker examines new tree growth in a replanted area.

Contents Page: Mother bison and calf on the prairie of the Tallgrass Prairie Preserve

PHOTO SOURCES

Cover Photo: © Harvey Payne
© Jeffrey Aronson/Network Aspen 39; Alberta Forestry, Lands, & Wildlife 81, 82; © Walt Anderson 61 middle, 74 left, 85, 87; Atlanta Trees 54; Bureau of Land Management 57; ©Haroldo Castro/Conservation International 86; © Photograph by Daniel Dancer 48, 65; John Deere Company 8; Steven Delaney, U.S. EPA 53; Dinodia Picture Agency 75; Photo by Adrian Dorst 80; Dye, Van Mol & Lawrence, Nashville, TN 77; Fermilab Visual Media Services 20 bottom, 34, 35 both; Cynthia Gehrie 11 right; Tiana Glenn/ Boise Interagency Fire Center 61 top left; © David Gordon 83; Carrol Henderson 6 left, 18 top, 19, 84 bottom, 90 top, 91; © Rick Jackson/Travel Montana 43; © Randall Hyman 44; Idaho National Panhandle Forest 51 bottom; Iowa Department of Natural Resources 21 both; The Kansas State Historical Society, Topeka, Kansas 13, 38 top; © Anne Keiser 45 left; © Gary Kramer 7; Justine Kushner 37 top; Lin Caufield Photographers 50 bottom; LowCountry ReLEAF 55; © Alexander Lowry, 1973 66, 67; © Dr. Alan Mallams 45 right; Mattole River Restoration Council 72, 73; State Archives of Michigan, neg. no. 00138 62; From the collection of the Minnesota Historical Society 23; © The Church of Jesus Christ of Latter-day Saints. Used by permission. 9; Charles Munn 90 bottom, Nebraska Department of Economic Development 26, 27; Ohio Department of Natural Resources 37 bottom; Photo by LuRay Parker, Wyoming Game & Fish Department 22 both; Courtesy of Parks Canada 42; © Harvey Payne 3, 5, 16; Probe International/Peggy Hallaward 88 bottom; © Robert Queen 46; © Eugene Schulz 1992 84 left; © Fred Siskind 40; Soil Conservation Service 24, 38 left; Al Stenstrup 18 bottom both, 60, 79; Photo by David Swanlund, courtesy of Save-the-Redwoods League 64; Targhee National Forest 20 top; The Land Institute 29 both, 31 both, 32; Lisa Turner 88 top; Melissa Turner 17, 41; UN Photo/Jackie Cartis 74 bottom; U.S. Fish & Wildlife Service/R.L. Herman 6 bottom; U.S. Fish & Wildlife Service 51 right; University of Wisconsin-Madison Arboretum 33; USDA Forest Service 1, 11 top, 50 right, 58, 61 right, 68, 69, 71; John Walters 28; Dan Weggeland, "Pioneers Cross the Plains 1862" © The Church of Jesus Christ of Latter-day Saints. Used by permission. 12; Weyerhauser 50 left; Terri Willis 56; Wind Cave National Park 4; Wisconsin Department of Natural Resources 63 both; Yellowstone National Park 70

CONTENTS

The Return of the Buffalo

The Earth trembled and shook. Pounding hooves raised clouds of dust. Three hundred huge, shaggy beasts thundered onto the open grassland of Oklahoma. For the first time in more than 100 years, buffalo were running free on the American tallgrass prairie.

It happened on October 18, 1993, when the buffalo were released onto the Tallgrass Prairie Preserve. The preserve was created by an organization called The Nature Conservancy.

The land had been a ranch for a long time, but it was once an open grassland—a prairie. The Nature Conservancy scientists chose land where native plants were already dominant. They are trying to restore "natural" conditions in several ways. They allow fires to happen naturally and control

restore = to return to the original condition.

As prairie lands disappeared, so did prairie dogs.

4

The Tallgrass Prairie Preserve in Oklahoma is part of the largest piece of native tallgrass prairie left in North America.

As many as 75 million buffalo may have lived on the North American plains when European settlers first arrived. Some restored prairies have buffalo herds on them once again.

the amount of grazing on the land. They encourage the growth of native plants and the return of native animals. They have begun by returning the magnificent buffalo.

The buffalo will feast on more than 500 species of prairie plants and grasses that now grow on the land. Soon, The Nature Conservancy hopes to have a herd of 1,400 buffalo roaming the preserve.

The release of the first 300 buffalo was a great event. A Native American plains tribe—the Osage—performed a buffalo welcoming ceremony. Then they and The Nature Conservancy members had a "prairie party." They invited local farmers, ranchers, and people who are concerned about the environment. Everyone celebrated the return of the buffalo.

A Land of Plenty

The buffalo, also called the American bison, is a symbol of the original prairie. It represents the native wildness and beauty of America. Once, tens of millions of buffalo lived on the vast prairie—a region of grasses called the Great Plains. They stretched from Illinois to eastern Montana and from Saskatchewan in Canada to central Texas. This huge grassland was home to prairie dogs, buffalo, countless birds, and American antelope, called pronghorns.

About 400 years ago, Europeans began coming to North America. They first settled in the East. At that time, most of eastern North America was covered with forests. The settlers cut down the forests to clear the land for farming, to build towns, and for fuel.

More settlers arrived and soon the East was crowded. New settlers headed West, seeking new land to farm. As they traveled, they crossed the endless, open grasslands of the prairie. But the flat plains looked strange and forbidding to them. So settlers rushed across the miles of open land.

Pronghorn used to roam the plains from Canada to Mexico.

7

Thousands of wagon trains traveled overland to western North America, carrying pioneer families. On the West Coast, too, settlers began to clear forests for farmland.

Before long, the West Coast became crowded with people. The only place left for farming was the prairie. So some new settlers moved to the plains. They plowed up the native grasses and planted crops. As you will see, the crops they planted were not good for the prairie.

Good-bye Grasslands

There is no prairie without prairie grasses. The roots of the grasses hold the prairie soil in place. Each year as new grasses grow, the old roots break apart and become part of the soil. Without native grasses, a plain is just flat land.

Prairie settlers plowed up the native grasses. Without plant roots to hold it down, the soil began

Settlers plowed the prairie to plant crops. There was nothing to hold the soil in place once the grass plants were gone.

to blow away in the strong winds or wash away with the rain. And after a few years of planting corn and wheat, the farmers found that the soil lost its richness. Crops dried up because the plains get very little rain. Before long, farmers on the plains could no longer make a living.

Good-bye Buffalo

Huge herds of buffalo used to roam the Great Plains of North America. Early settlers saw buffalo herds that were one mile (1.6 kilometers) wide and stretched for miles. Settlers told how they had to wait five days for one herd of buffalo to pass by their wagons.

Millions of buffalo were slaughtered. The writing on this buffalo skull shows the distance traveled by one group of pioneers who crossed the plains in 1847.

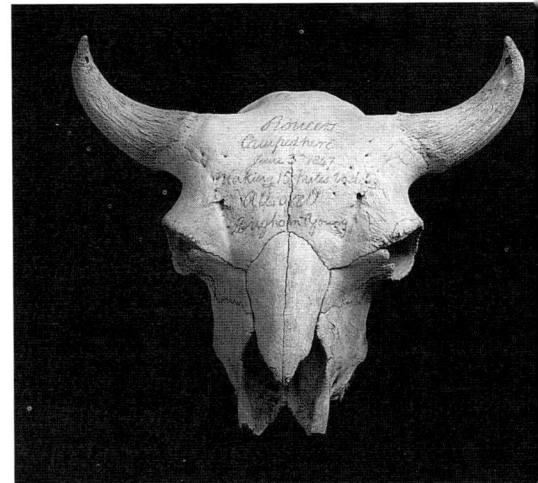

When settlers began farming the plains, war was declared on the buffalo. People decided that there wasn't room on the land for both farmers and buffalo. In the late 1800s, the government encouraged people to kill the animals.

In less than 20 years, tens of millions of buffalo were killed. Some were shot for their fur. Some were shot for their tongues, which people liked to eat. Some were shot just for "fun." During these years, the rotting bodies of dead buffalo dotted the landscape.

Other prairie animals, including pronghorns and prairie dogs, also died. As the plow tore up the native grasses, prairie animals no longer had food. The natural world of the prairie was finished. But today, people are working to restore some prairie to the way it was before settlers came.

Good-bye Forests

Most North American forests suffered too. The settlers cut the trees down to make room for farmland. Lumber companies chopped down trees to sell the wood. Soon, animals that once roamed the forest, such as lynx, mountain lions, and wolves, began to disappear.

Today, many of the original American forests have been reduced in size. Forests on other continents also are disappearing rapidly. Many people now are working to protect the forests that remain and to restore some that have been destroyed.

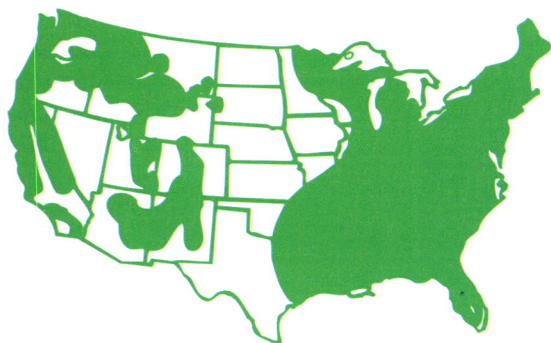

Original Forests 1620

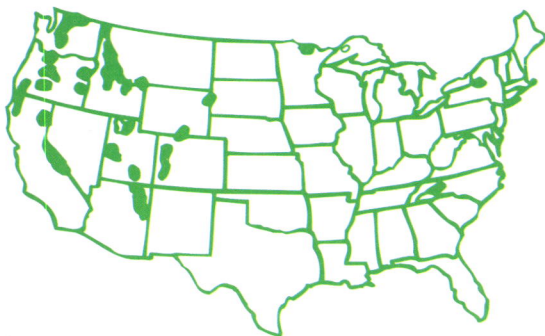

Original Forests 1990

Restoring the Earth

People today understand more about how to use the land without harming it. We see the mistakes our ancestors made, and we want to stop others from making the same mistakes.

But we also know that people must use the land. We need food to eat, so farmers must grow crops. We need wood for houses, furniture, and

paper. And people need to earn money from the land they own.

People who care about the Earth and its living things are working hard to find a balance between human needs and the needs of nature. One way to do that is by restoring the land to its natural condition.

Neither prairie nor forest can be restored completely, however. There are just too many people living on Earth now. But some people are succeeding in restoring prairie and forest lands. In this book, you will read about people who are working to protect the prairies and forests we still have and to bring these important parts of our environment back to life.

Forest Service workers prepare to reseed a logged forest area (top). A child is planting wildflowers called blazing stars at a restored prairie site in Illinois (above).

The Story of the Prairie

For weeks their covered wagons bumped and rolled through what seemed like a sea of grass. The grass towered ten feet (3 meters) high in some places. The pioneers had to climb on top of their wagons to see over the tops of the tall plants. They looked for a landmark—a tree, a hill—but all they saw was an endless sea of swaying grass. To pioneers heading for the West Coast, the prairie was an empty and unfriendly place.

Long lines of covered wagons moved slowly across the Great Plains in the 1800s.

The Great Plains were the last region of the United States to be settled. In 1862, the government passed the Homestead Act, offering free prairie land to settlers who would move there and farm the land. Pioneers soon began to move into this harsh and beautiful place.

Dryness and Wind

Prairies are in-between places. There is usually a moist forest on one side and a dry desert on the other. Few trees can grow there. On the prairie, grass is king. Prairies are generally dry places where rainfall is rare and unreliable. In North America, the prairie gets drier as you move from east to west.

1 Shortgrass Prairie

Lime Layer

Soil Always Dry

2 Mixed or Middle

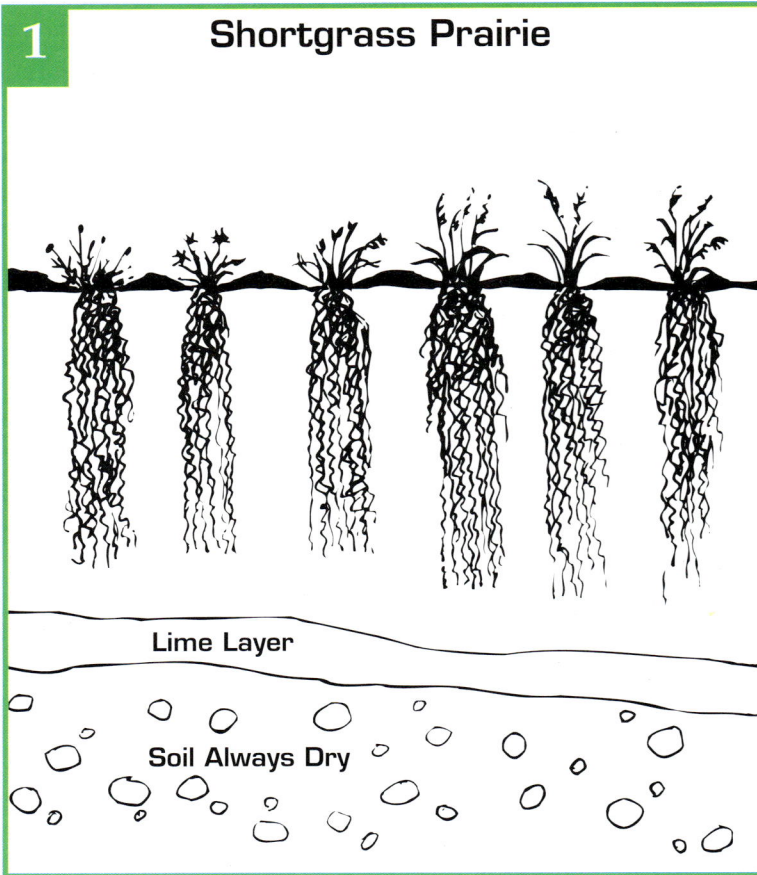

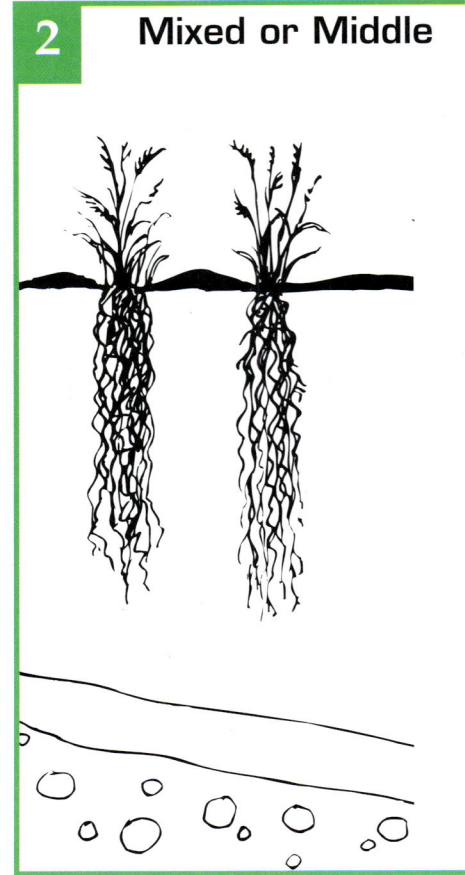

Cross sections of prairie types from the west (left) to the east (right). Mixed grass prairie covers the most land.

The eastern prairie gets up to 35 inches (89 centimeters) of rain a year—enough to soak the deep roots of the ten-foot (3-meter) grasses, such as big bluestem. This is the land of the tallgrass prairie.

Medium-sized grasses, such as little bluestem, grow a little farther west where there is less rain. It covers the largest land area. The western part of the prairie east of the Rocky Mountains often gets less than ten inches (25 centimeters) of rain a year. Short grasses, such as five-inch- (12.5-centimeter-)

Grass Prairie

3 Tallgrass Prairie

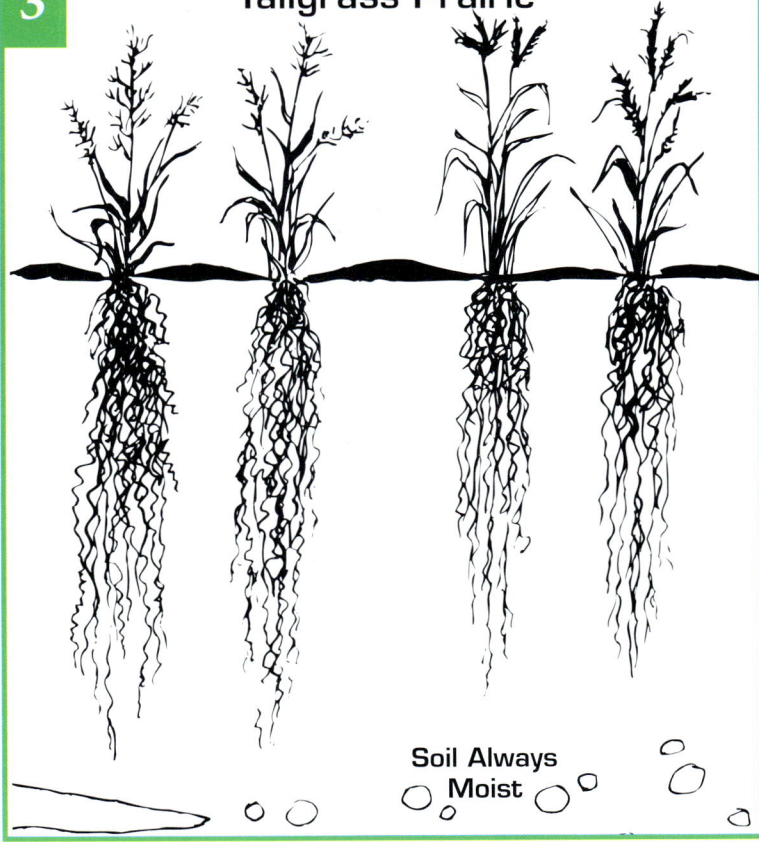

Soil Always Moist

tall buffalo grass, grow on this part of the prairie.

Native prairie grasses can survive dry weather and extreme cold. Their roots grow deep into the earth where the soil stays moist and doesn't freeze.

Prairies are also windy places. Prairies are generally flat and open with gently rolling hills. There is usually nothing to block the fierce winds that batter and bend the grasses. The howling winds suck moisture from the soil, leaving even less water for the plants.

Fire is important in maintaining a healthy prairie. New prairie grasses thrive after a fire. The underground roots are not destroyed.

A Place of Fire

From spring through fall, violent storms often lash the plains. Sometimes they bring tornadoes, but usually they bring lightning. Lightning bolts crash out of thunderclouds to strike the flat, dry grassland, often setting it on fire.

Fire was called "red buffalo" by Native Americans of the plains. Prairie fires "stampede" over the dry grasses burning everything in their path. High winds may whip the flames into a "fire blizzard." Walls of flame 30 feet (9 meters) high sweep over the plains faster than a horse can gallop. With a deep roar, fire quickly can reduce vast regions of prairie to ashes.

It is true that some animals are unable to escape such fires. Yet without fire, the prairie and its wildlife could not continue to exist. How can such terrible fires help the prairie?

Friendly Fire

The most important part of a prairie lies underground where plant roots enrich the soil. Fire burns the tops of grasses, but their roots survive. After a fire, the roots put out more shoots than they do normally. So prairie grasses flourish after they are burned.

Without fire, the dead grasses pile up year after year, gradually choking new growth. Fire frees the nutrients, such as minerals found in both living and dead plants. The soil takes in the nutrients and becomes richer and healthier. Burning the grasses also allows sunlight to reach the soil.

nutrients = the chemical substances plants and animals need to live and grow.

Trees cannot grow on the prairie because of dryness, wind, and fire. There is not enough water for trees to grow on the prairie. The powerful prairie wind keeps trees from growing properly. Also, grass grows back after a fire much more quickly than a tree can. The quickly sprouting grass prevents trees from growing after a fire.

New plant shoots sprout from the ground after a prairie fire, making the prairie new again (left).

Prairie flowers such as the blazing star (below) and brown-eyed susans (below right) are often stopping places for beautiful butterflies (right).

The Rich Soil

For thousands of years, grasses covered the plains like a green blanket. Grass roots spread and held the soil in place. Dead grasses rotted on the ground, enriching the soil. Occasionally fire burned the grasses, giving the soil healthful nutrients. New grasses and wildflowers flourished. Insects, especially butterflies, were drawn to the many wildflowers. The colorful butterflies and blossoms made the prairie very beautiful.

Over time, these natural processes made prairie soil the richest and healthiest soil on Earth.

The Soil Keepers

Animals that live on the prairie help keep it fertile. Many small prairie animals live in holes in the ground called burrows. There they are safe from their enemies. Mice, ground squirrels, badgers, and the burrowing owl all live in burrows. The burrows of prairie dogs are like tunnels in a huge subway system. They are called prairie dog "towns."

When an animal digs a burrow, the deep soil is loosened and turned up. Air and the nutrients from rotting plants on the surface mix with the soil and add to its richness.

Buffalo had an important role in keeping the grasslands fertile. They moved from place to place, nibbling on the sweet grasses. The animals' droppings added nutrients to the soil. The buffalo also helped control fire. Areas of chewed down grasses didn't burn well and often stopped fires from spreading too far.

fertile = very rich and able to support life.

Badgers live in burrows just as prairie dogs do.

Animals in the Grass

Pronghorns are graceful grazing animals of the plains. The fastest animals in North America, they can run 70 miles (113 kilometers) per hour for up to four minutes. Pronghorns depend on their great speed to escape danger.

19

Elk have left the prairie to find safety in the forests.

When farmers began cultivating the land, the prairie chicken population fell.

Many prairie animals are protected by their colors. Baby pronghorns lie still, curled up among the grasses on the brown earth of the prairie. They are hard to see, and so are protected from the fox, coyote, and other hunters.

Elk and bighorn sheep once lived on the prairies too. But the elk have moved into the safer forests, and bighorn sheep now are found mainly in desert country.

If you visit the plains in the spring, you may hear a strange booming sound. It is the mating call of the male grouse, or prairie chicken. Female grouse love to hear the males "boom." After mating, the females make nests and lay eggs in the tall grass. The eggs—light brown with dark brown spots—blend in with the soil and the grass.

Other prairie birds, such as sandpipers and killdeer, are also brown. They are almost invisible when sitting on their ground nests.

Many kinds of mice and voles are hunted by meat-eating animals. Hawks and golden eagles swoop down on careless mice, killing them with their claws. They rip the flesh apart with their strong beaks. Weasels, badgers, and other meat eaters also hunt prairie mice.

Making a Start with Switchgrass

When farmers planted switchgrass, many birds returned to nest in Iowa. The state government helped farmers plant switchgrass because most of the original grasslands had become farmland. Birds that needed native grasses had no place to live.

Switchgrass grows up to six feet (1.8 meters) tall. Ring-necked pheasants (top left) and bobwhite quail nested on the ground among the tall grasses. So did warblers, sparrows, and mourning doves. Meadowlarks made their nests out of grass.

The state government's plan helped the farmers as well as the birds. They fed the switchgrass to their cattle (top right)!

This successful state program ended in 1986 after Iowa farmers had planted thousands of acres in switchgrass. The federal government began a new program, the Prairie Preserve Program, that preserves many more acres of prairie than a state program can. But Iowa had the right idea!

Return of the Ferrets

In Wyoming black-footed ferrets have been released from special cages back into the prairie habitat where they once thrived.

Black-footed ferrets were hunters on the short-grass prairie. Their favorite meal was prairie dogs. When the Great Plains were settled, ranchers tried to get rid of prairie dogs because they ate grass needed to feed cattle. Also, the cattle sometimes tripped in prairie dog burrows.

When prairie dogs disappeared from most of the Great Plains, the ferrets starved. Soon, most of them were gone. Black-footed ferrets were among the first animals listed as endangered. In fact, scientists thought these animals were extinct.

Then, in 1981, a dog on a Wyoming ranch killed a strange animal. It turned out to be a black-footed ferret! Scientists immediately started searching for more of these endangered animals. They found 130 ferrets.

endangered = in danger of dying out completely; almost extinct, or no longer in existence.

In 1985, the ferrets got a terrible disease. Most of them died. Scientists took the few surviving ferrets to a wildlife center. Soon the ferrets mated, and slowly their numbers increased.

Some black-footed ferrets have been returned to the wild near a prairie dog town outside Veteran, Wyoming. Ranchers in the area have agreed not to harm the prairie dogs or the ferrets.

22

Scientists would like to release more ferrets back into the wild. But most prairie dog towns are empty today. By restoring shortgrass prairie and returning the prairie dogs to it, we can give black-footed ferrets their wild home once again. Only then will this endangered prairie animal survive.

Settlers on the Plains

In the late 1800s, white settlers came to the prairie. "Experts" had insisted that the prairie soil wouldn't grow good crops, but the settlers were willing to try.

Their first task was "breaking" the sod—the tough soil and matted roots near the surface—to prepare it for planting. Sod busting, as it was called, sliced away all the grass on top of the soil. It also broke up the roots underground. It often took 14 oxen to pull a plow through unbroken prairie sod.

sod = prairie soil held together in a solid mat by grass roots.

The prairie sod was so strong that blocks of it were used to build homes for settlers.

drought = a period of little or no rainfall.

After the grasses were plowed under, seeds were planted, and the first crops began to grow. And how they grew! The fertile prairie soil produced the best crops of corn and wheat the farmers had ever seen. As word spread, more and more settlers flocked to the Great Plains to farm.

Boom . . . and Bust

Soon, grains such as corn and wheat covered thousands of square miles of what was once wild grassland. Americans stopped thinking of the prairie as a "sea of grass." It became "the breadbasket of the world."

During these early years, rainfall was plentiful. The farmers had no idea that the weather of the 1870s was unusual.

After a few years, things began to go wrong. The crops were not as abundant. The grass roots that once held the soil in place and made it fertile had been plowed up and destroyed. The nutrients in the soil were used up.

And the rain had stopped falling. Drought rules the plains in most years, and periods of good rainfall are very rare. The soil dried out and began to blow away during windstorms. The grains farmers planted had shallow roots. When the soil dried, the roots dried out, too. Crops died from lack of water before they could be harvested. The sun beat down on the naked earth, turning it to dust.

By the 1930s, unwise farming and drought had turned the soil to dust over vast areas of the southern plains. Strong winds blew across the plains, sweeping up clouds of dry soil. The sky darkened as the air filled with choking dust. What had once been rich farmland had become a "Dust Bowl."

The Plains in Trouble

All over the Great Plains, farmers left their ruined land. Those who stayed behind discovered they could get water by digging deep wells. They pumped the water to the surface from an underground source called an aquifer. For tens of thousands of years, rainwater has been collecting in the aquifers.

The farmers had discovered the giant Ogallala

aquifer = an underground area of rock and sand that collects water that seeps through the soil after rain.

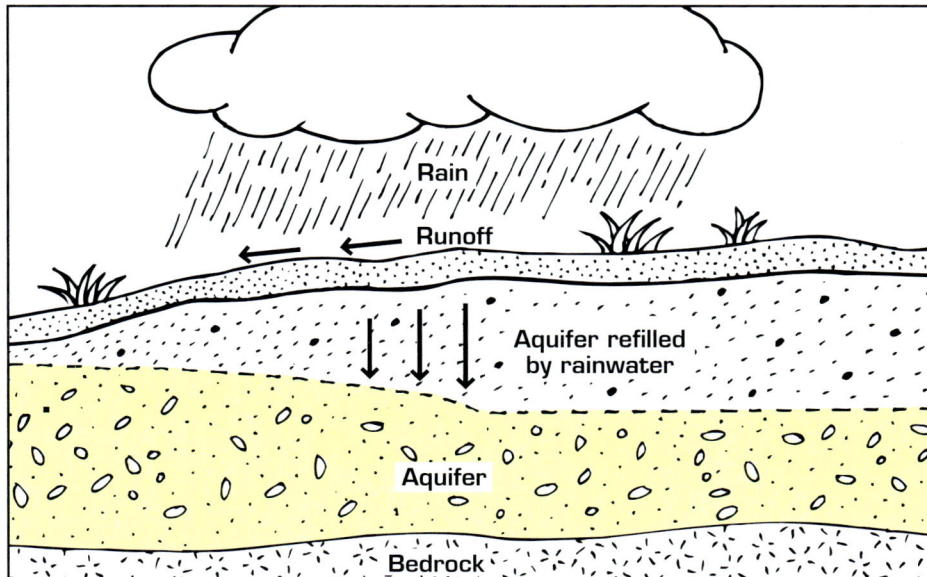

Rain

Runoff

Aquifer refilled by rainwater

Aquifer

Bedrock

Looking from the outskirts of Lincoln, Nebraska, toward the Great Plains

Aquifer, named after a Native American tribe. The aquifer lies under much of the Great Plains, including North and South Dakota, Nebraska, Kansas, Colorado, Oklahoma, Wyoming, and Texas. People in these states get their water from the Ogallala Aquifer.

Farm by farm, and state by state, more and more people dug wells down into the Ogallala Aquifer. Growing cities and industries added to the constant drain. Today, billions of gallons of water are pumped out of the aquifer every year.

People use water for their crops and livestock. They use it in factories and for drinking.

Unfortunately, people take more water out of the aquifer than rain puts back in. In 1950, the aquifer under Kansas was 58 feet (18 meters) deep. Today, it is only six feet (1.8 meters) deep in many places. The Ogallala Aquifer is expected to run out of water soon after the year 2000.

What will plains people drink then? How will they water their crops? What will happen to this "breadbasket" that feeds so much of the world?

Bringing Back the Prairies

The pioneers used to tell a story about an elder of the Sioux people who saw a farmer plowing up prairie sod. The Sioux bent down and thoughtfully examined the plowed earth. Looking up at the farmer, he said, "Wrong side up."

The pioneers who told this story thought the joke was on the Sioux. Today, we know the joke was on the farmer. The Sioux was right. Plowing up the grass roots that enrich the prairie soil is definitely "wrong side up." The Sioux understood that roots under the ground should stay there because they make the prairie soil fertile. As author and farmer Wendell Berry has said, "We plowed the prairies and never knew what we were doing, because we never knew what we were undoing."

For years, North American people have depended on the crops grown by the farmers of the prairie states and Canadian provinces. Most of these crops are grains such as wheat and corn. While wheat and corn are grasses, they are very different from native prairie grasses. Why does one kind of grass enrich the prairie soil and another kind of grass destroy it?

These farmers are harvesting hay on the plains.

This question puzzled scientist and prairie lover Wes Jackson. Was there some way to develop grasses that would both provide food and restore the prairie? He started a research institute, The Land Institute, and assembled a team of scientists to try to answer that question. His institute is on the plains of Kansas.

At first glance, you might think Wes Jackson's problem is easy to solve. But the laws of nature sometimes do not meet the needs of people. Wes Jackson is trying to create a kind of grass that not only puts down deep roots but also produces many seeds. With prairie plants and grasses, it doesn't happen often.

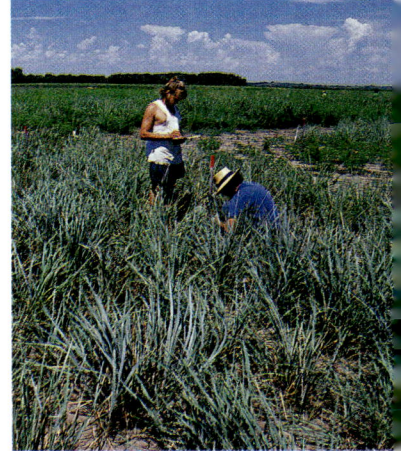

Wes Jackson (left) started The Land Institute in Kansas to find ways to help both people and the prairie. Wild rye (above) is one of the grasses being studied.

Different Kinds of Grasses

Like all green plants, native prairie grasses use the energy from sunlight to make the food they need. Prairie grasses use most of this energy to grow deep roots. They have little energy left to produce many seeds.

Grains, the grasses we grow for food, also get their energy from sunlight. But they use most of this energy to produce seeds. We grind these wheat grains for flour and eat the kernels of corn.

Unfortunately, grain plants have little energy left over for growing roots. So food grains have shallow roots that cannot survive drought and cold. Every winter the roots die, making the plants unable to send up new shoots. Each spring, farmers must plow the earth again and plant new grain seeds.

Wes Jackson's ideal grain will have both deep roots and many seeds. This kind of crop will make plowing every year unnecessary. Its roots will survive drought and cold, keep the soil fertile, and hold it in place. And, like

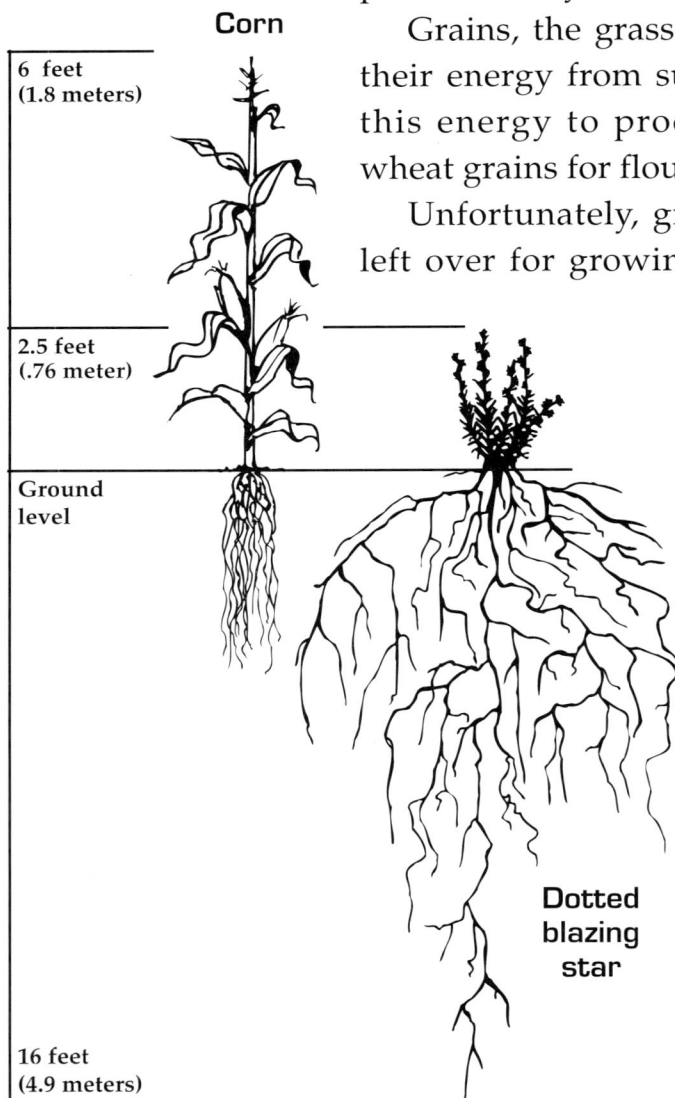

Corn

6 feet
(1.8 meters)

2.5 feet
(.76 meter)

Ground
level

**Dotted
blazing
star**

16 feet
(4.9 meters)

other grain crops, it will produce similar amounts of seeds.

Creating a New Kind of Grain

The Land Institute works with eastern gama grass—a deep-rooted native prairie grass. In one

Eastern gama grass

experiment, Wes Jackson developed a kind of gama grass that produces four times as many seeds as normal gama grass.

Like most natural environments, native prairies contain many different kinds of plants. On one part of the Institute land, scientists have planted an interesting mix of plants. Here, eastern gama grass, a giant wild rye grass sent to Kansas from Russia, and a relative of the bean plant called Illinois bundleflower grow together. The three plants live well together and produce many seeds.

Elsewhere in the fields, The Land Institute is

Milo, also known as sorghum, is a relative of corn.

31

growing an entirely new plant. Researchers began with milo, a seed-rich food grain that must be newly planted every year. They crossbred the milo with Johnson grass, a plant that survives from year to year. The scientists are still experimenting with this new plant. Maybe it will become the many-seeded, deep-rooted grain they are looking for.

Wes Jackson is trying to develop a way of farming that may restore the prairie. What is needed, he says, "is to ask what nature requires of people here rather than posing the childish question, 'What can we get away with?' "

Shown here is a crossbred grass produced from milo and Johnson grass.

Particles and Prairies

Just outside Chicago, deep underground, a group of scientists study the strange ways of atoms. They zoom atoms at amazing speeds around a hollow ring four miles (6.4 kilometers) long. When the atoms crash into each other, they shatter into particles that scientists can study.

This underground atom smasher is named Fermilab after Enrico Fermi, a famous atomic scientist. When Fermilab was established, the land above it was covered by scraggly weeds. Plant scientists from a nearby college asked Fermilab if they could try to restore the land to native prairie. Fermilab agreed. The experiment, which began in

1974, was patterned after a 60-acre (24-hectare) prairie at the University of Wisconsin that had been restored since the 1930s.

From the Bottom Up

Robert Betz teaches biology at a university in Illinois. When he's not in the classroom, he's out restoring prairie. He and people from The Nature Conservancy began work on a small part of the Fermilab land. The first thing they did was plow. And they plowed over and over again. They hoped that all their plowing would destroy the weeds that covered the land.

Then Betz and his crew of helpers began looking for native prairie seeds. This was no simple task. Illinois is called the Prairie State. But of the

Greene Prairie at the University of Wisconsin showed other people that prairie could be restored.

original 40,000 square miles (103,000 square kilometers) of tallgrass prairie in Illinois, only four square miles (10 square kilometers) remain today.

Betz and his volunteers searched for small patches of untouched prairie where the original grasses still grew. Such land is found mainly in old cemeteries and along railroad tracks. They collected 400 pounds (181 kilograms) of seeds from over 70 different prairie grasses and wildflowers. Then they planted them carefully.

What do you think came up? Weeds! Millions of weeds! But Robert Betz wasn't discouraged. He knew that prairie is created from the bottom up where the plants put down deep roots.

"Sure enough," he said, "in the second year, all of a sudden these little fellows started to grow." After three years, the grasses above Fermilab were thick enough to burn in a controlled prairie fire that "rolled over those weeds and cleared 'em all out."

Each year, more Fermilab land was restored. By 1983 tons of native plant seeds were collected from the restored sections and used to seed the remaining land. Today, Fermilab prairie is the largest restored prairie in the United States.

A volunteer gathers prairie-grass seeds in the Fermilab restored prairie. Wilson Hall, the central laboratory building, is visible in the background.

Fermilab prairie is a success—or the start of a success. It has been said, "You can destroy a prairie in two hours. But to rebuild it might take half a century or more." It will still take perhaps 30 to 50 years for the restored native grasses to build the deep root system found in original prairie.

Robert Betz and other scientists also are preparing to bring native wildlife to the Fermilab prairie. Cranes, swans, ground squirrels, and even prairie insects are being introduced. Prairie birds such as meadowlarks, bobolinks, and falcons already have moved in on their own. And, yes, the Fermilab prairie also will get its own small herd of buffalo.

Visitors enjoy the prairie interpretive trail at Fermilab (above). Each year, the grasses on the restored prairie get stronger (below).

Kid Power Helps Create Prairie!

Aaron is a Boy Scout who lives in a town in Kansas that is probably a lot like your town. It has many houses, stores, highways, and shopping malls.

Aaron is interested in the environment. As a Boy Scout project, he decided to help restore one of the town's parks to native prairie. He rounded up 30 other Boy Scouts and their fathers. After getting permission, they began the hard work of clearing a section of the park as big as a football field.

Aaron and his friends cleared the area of bushes, weeds, and even poison ivy! When they finished their work, the county parks department moved in. First, they burned the cleared field. Then they seeded it with native prairie grasses.

When asked how he kept his volunteers happy while they worked so hard, Aaron's answer was smart and simple. "I brought potato chips and cookies," he said.

Is It the Real Thing?

Scientists believe that even the best-restored prairie never will be exactly like the original. Weeds and other plants brought to the area by settlers may never be wiped out totally. And because plants compete for space to grow just as animals compete for space to live, these foreign plants may make it impossible for some native plants to grow.

When restoring a prairie, the first seeds planted are those of native prairie grasses that can compete with weeds. After a few years, these strong plants choke out most of the weeds. Once the strong plants are growing, scientists add the seeds of weaker prairie plants. They hope these weaker plants can compete with the few remaining weeds. However, a few prairie plants are not strong enough to compete. These plants need special attention until they can re-establish themselves.

In addition, certain prairie orchids and daisies are endangered because their environment has changed. The strict regulation of fire and the number of grazing cattle have put them at risk of extinction. Scientists are trying to find a way to help them grow on restored prairie.

Non-native trees that block growth of native prairie are cleared (above). The prairie fringed orchid (below) reaches two feet (60 centimeters) high.

Professor Popper's Plan

People who live on the vast, dry Great Plains call it "next year country." When asked what this means, they smile and shake their heads. "Next year we'll get better crops. Next year we won't owe money. Next year it will rain," they say. Unfortunately, "next year" almost never comes.

Frank Popper teaches land-use planning at a New Jersey college. On his way home one day, he got stuck in traffic. Instead of becoming irritated, Professor Popper began thinking about a problem

Ghost towns in Kansas (top) and deserted farms (above) are common sights in the Great Plains.

that had been on his mind for some time—the future of the Great Plains.

Conditions on the Great Plains are harsh. Little rain means poor crops. Soil has been ruined by farming and cattle grazing. Large ranches and farms have survived the changing weather and economy better than small farms. Many people have had to leave the plains they love because they could no longer make a living. They have found jobs in the cities or moved to better farmland elsewhere. Kansas has more than 800 ghost towns, and Nebraska has about 10,000 deserted farmhouses.

The Buffalo Commons

Professor Popper realized that the way things are going, the Great Plains may become a wasteland of ruined soil. But he has a bold and daring plan to restore the Great Plains. He calls it the

Buffalo Commons. This plan would restore short-grass prairie and herds of buffalo to plains counties where few people live.

At last count, 143 Great Plains counties had fewer than two people per square mile (2.5 square kilometers). The region had the same number of people when it was "empty" frontier. Professor Popper believes the region and its people might be saved if 139,000 square miles (360,010 square kilometers) of failing farms and dying towns in these counties were restored to native prairie.

Professor Frank Popper and his wife Deborah pose for a photograph on the prairie in Hayes County, Nebraska.

The Buffalo Commons would be created gradually. Thriving towns and farms would be left alone. But those towns and farms that can't survive would be allowed to fade away. "Then," Frank Popper says, "the government will take the newly empty plains and tear down the fences. It will plant shortgrass prairie. It will bring in native animals, especially the buffalo."

We'll Never Agree!

When they first heard about the Buffalo Commons, the plains people were furious. "How dare a college professor from the East tell us what to do!" they raged. Today, Frank Popper tours the plains states and explains his idea to the people.

"We are not talking about buffalo on every acre, or removing farmers and ranchers by force," he says. "We are talking about a gradual change that will help people in the region. They will make a living through conservation, buffalo, and tourists. It will be a new way of thinking about the plains."

Not Such a Bad Idea, After All

Plains people are starting to consider Frank Popper's plan. Some realize he might be more than "a crazy man from the East who wants to kick us out and replace us with buffalo." More people have seen that an idea like the Buffalo Commons can save the land and help them too.

They have seen that national parks and wilderness areas in the West are doing well. These areas attract tourists and create jobs for people.

The Buffalo Commons would help the Great Plains in the same way. Tourism would help the economy. Tourists would come to see the wide-open beauty of the prairie and the free-roaming buffalo. They would watch prairie dogs and pronghorns. And they would see the Wild West prairie as the pioneers saw it.

Frank Popper believes that parts of the plains can continue to be a "breadbasket." In some areas wheat and new kinds of grain can be grown. Farmers will plant crops that suit the land and climate of the prairie.

The Buffalo Commons would attract tourists just as Yellowstone National Park in Wyoming does.

Coming to a Supermarket Near You...

In 1986, South Dakota rancher Duane Lammers began the American Bison Association. (Bison is another name for buffalo.) Mr. Lammers got rid of his cattle and started raising buffalo on his ranch. Today, 1,500 buffalo graze on his 24,000-acre (9,700-hectare) ranch. He sells some of the buffalo for meat. Others have become movie stars! Some of Mr. Lammers's buffalo appeared in the movie *Dances With Wolves.*

Buffalo meat is already on sale at supermarkets in the West. It has become so popular that the demand for buffalo meat is greater now than the supply. So buffalo ranchers are expanding their herds. More and more ranchers are raising buffalo. If the buffalo have enough room to graze, they will help, not hurt, the land. Then their tasty meat will please food shoppers, too. Buffalo also will eat the dry prairie grasses in winter, while cattle must be given feed. And buffalo eat a wider range of prairie plants than cattle do. Buffalo burgers anyone?

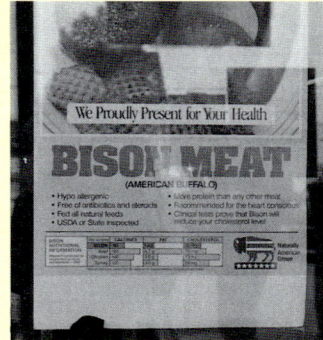

The Buffalo Commons would fit in well with the deep-rooted, seed-rich plants that Wes Jackson is trying to develop. Farmers who plant deep-rooted crops would not need underground water. These deep-rooted plants hold water for a long time and they can survive drought. Thus, what remains of the Ogallala Aquifer also would be preserved for future generations.

When it is complete, Grasslands National Park in Canada will cover 350 square miles (906 square kilometers) of native and restored prairie. It also may have herds of buffalo.

A Canadian "Buffalo Commons"

In 1981, after many years of planning, the Canadian government began creating Grasslands National Park in the Great Plains of the province of Saskatchewan. Many Canadian ranchers and farmers like the idea of restoring the grasslands and preserving them in a park. They, too, have had a hard time raising animals and crops on their worn-out land.

The Canadian government is buying up farms and ranches from people willing to sell. Farmers and ranchers sometimes make more money selling their property than working on the land. The government then will restore the land to native prairie.

Many Canadian farmers and ranchers are eager to see Grasslands National Park created. They are pushing the government to buy up land more quickly. They want their land restored to native prairie as soon as possible.

The Big Open

Eastern Montana is a land of cowboys and cattle. For many years, ranchers grazed too many cattle on the short grasses of these dry plains. The cattle ate the grass all the way down to the roots so it could not grow back. The soil began to suffer and ranchers were losing money. Overgrazing was ruining the plains.

Eastern Montana is also prime prairie country. In the mid-1980s, Robert Scott of the Institute of the Rockies in Missoula, Montana, had an idea. He suggested that ranchers get together to restore the prairie and make money at the same time. His plan called for a huge preserve called the Big Open. It would be large enough to support tens of thousands of buffalo, deer, elk, and antelope.

Land that becomes part of the Big Open still would be owned by ranchers. They would make money selling permits to visitors who wanted to hike, camp, or hunt on their land.

Thousands of new jobs could be created in the area. People could work in stores that sell outdoor equipment. They could work as wilderness guides. They could work in motels, restaurants, and gas stations.

If all the ranchers join, the Big Open one day may be 15,000 square miles (38,850 square kilometers) of natural prairie.

The vast prairie lands of eastern Montana someday may become a preserve called the Big Open.

The Shortgrass Steppes

steppe = open, dry, flat land with short grasses, especially the plains of Russia and Ukraine.

The grasslands of Russia and Ukraine are called steppes. These flat lands covered with short grasses stretch across Ukraine, through southern Russia, and into central Asia. Like the North American prairie, the steppes were very fertile. Unfortunately, these grasslands were used as unwisely as ours were. And like us, Russian and Ukrainian farmers ruined the soil by destroying native grasses and planting the wrong crops.

This large farm on the steppes of Ukraine produces wheat.

Communist leaders tried to force the ruined land to produce too much food. They dumped tons of chemical plant food and insecticide on the steppes. Today, millions of acres of farmland are ruined. Thousands of tons of soil have blown away. What soil remains is poisoned with chemicals. The food grown on this poisoned soil sometimes makes people sick.

Some people are trying to save the steppes. A group called the Association for Ecology and Peace has made the Russian and Ukrainian people and governments realize the extent of the problem. Scientists and ordinary people have come together to change the way food is grown. They want the steppes restored to natural, healthy environment.

Saving Savannas

In parts of Africa and in some tropical lands, grasslands are called savannas. These areas are covered with coarse grasses and a few scattered trees. People from all over the world visit the savannas of East Africa to see the magnificent wildlife.

In East African countries, the tourist industry is very important. So these countries are trying to save the savannas and their animals. Large regions of savanna have been turned into national parks where animals, such as lions and cheetahs, are pro-

savanna = a tropical or subtropical grassland with coarse grasses and a few scattered trees.

Tourism is very important in Africa. Visitors come to the savanna of Tanzania's Serengeti Plain to watch and photograph wildlife such as giraffes (left) and lions (below).

tected. Tourists come to see these big cats hunt zebra, impala, and other animals on the grassland.

At first, preserving such vast areas of grassland was hard for the African countries. Many poor people wanted to use the savannas to grow food and graze their cattle. The African governments solved this problem by giving some money from the tourist industry to native people who live near the national parks. This money helps the people survive.

Is It Too Late?

It's not too late for the people of Africa to preserve their savannas. But in North America, the most we can do now is try to restore sections of prairie wherever possible.

The same is true for forests. As you saw on the maps on page 10, most of the original forests in the United States have been cut down. We can try to save what's left. We can try to restore some forests. But it's not too late for the people of Africa and South America to try to rescue their native forests.

As we will see in the next chapters, restoring forests can be lot harder than restoring prairies. But, in some ways, restoring forests is even more important.

Children run through the grasses of a prairie.

Saving and Creating Prairies

The Missouri Prairie Foundation, established in 1968, was the first local group to save native prairie. The group has more than 1,600 members who raise money to buy areas of untouched prairie. Their efforts have saved more than 1,000 acres (405 hectares) of prairie from destruction. The group also helps people turn their land—lawns, gardens, farms, or backyards—into tiny patches of prairie.

To create a prairie in your backyard or on an empty lot (and to create your own Success Story), follow the steps below.

1. Buy seeds from a company that sells native prairie grass seeds. The Missouri Prairie Foundation (see the end of the book for their address) can tell you where to buy your seeds.

2. Plow up the soil of your lawn or empty lot.

3. Scatter the native prairie seeds over the plowed soil.

4. Wait a while for the prairie grasses to grow.

You will be very pleased with your personal patch of prairie. It will attract birds and wildlife. It will grow beautifully year after year. You never will have to water it. You never will have to mow it.

Don't feel bad if you don't live on the Great Plains. You still can plant native grasses and plants around your house. Call your local Cooperative Extension to find out how to turn your lawn into a patch of native plants.

Into the Forests

"Fasten your safety belts! We're goin' up!" The engine roars, lifting you into the clouds. You're in a small airplane soaring above the mountainous national forests of the Pacific Northwest. You look down, expecting to see green mountains carpeted with 500-year-old forests. But that is not what you see.

The land below you looks like the surface of the moon—bare, gray slopes with no signs of life. This is exactly what the pilot has brought you to see.

The volunteer pilot works for Lighthawk, an environmental group. He tells you that nearly all

From the air, a clear-cut area of forest looks like a scar on the land.

the forests of these mountains and valleys have been stripped bare by logging. In loggers' terms, they have been clear-cut.

clear-cut = stripped bare of all trees, bushes, and other growth. Clear-cut land is usually burned after it is cut.

Lighthawk was started by a pilot named Michael Stewartt. He says, "I made up the name Lighthawk. I imagined a magical bird that shines light wherever it goes. And that's sort of what we do at Lighthawk. We take people up in planes. Then they can see clearly what is happening to the land. They really can see the problems."

Lighthawk pilots have flown government officials, TV and newspaper reporters, and environmental groups over areas destroyed by logging. Lighthawk has helped Americans see what is happening to their national forests. The sight of clear-cut ancient forests makes Michael Stewartt mad. He hopes his passengers will get angry, too.

Trees are a renewable resource—we can use them and they grow back. But we have been using up trees faster than we have replaced them, because the easiest and cheapest way to get the lumber from a forest is to clear-cut. In a clear-cut, every tree—big or little, old or young—is cut down. Without trees, the animals disappear. It takes many years for the forest to regrow. Some forests may never recover.

Another way to get wood out of forests is to cut down some trees—but not all of them—so that the other life is not disturbed terribly. This process is called selective cutting. Selective cutting requires

selective cutting = cutting down some trees while leaving others standing, as opposed to clear-cutting.

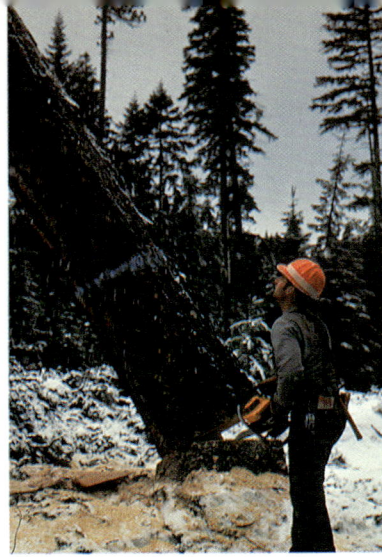

When a forest is clear-cut, all the trees are taken at once (left). In selective cutting, trees of different ages and types are cut while others are left standing (right).

more time and money, but it is usually better for the forest and the animals that live there.

Why Save Forests?

Look around you. What do you see that comes from forests? You probably see many things. The paper in this book is made from forest trees. So are paper towels, bags, newspapers, and cardboard boxes. Our houses, furniture, toys, baseball bats, and countless other items are made of wood. Do we need to preserve forests in order to continue to use products made from trees? Why else should we protect and rebuild the forests?

Forests are home to many kinds of plants and animals. And all these plants and animals are connected to each other in the web of forest life. For example, an oak tree may be a nesting place for chickadees. The chickadees eat insects that feed on oak leaves.

Many products such as baseball bats are made from wood.

Other birds eat caterpillars that munch tree leaves. Small animals hunt and eat the birds. The oak provides shade for berry bushes growing beneath it. Bears, birds, and other animals eat the delicious berries.

It is no surprise that destroying large areas of forest often leads to the near extinction of an animal or plant. For example, the northern spotted owl is threatened. It needs a forest of big, old trees to survive. Nearly all of its old-growth forest in the Northwest has been clear-cut.

old-growth forest = forest that has never been cut.

Sometimes trees can become "too old," or overmature. Because they are large, these old trees are worth a great deal of money. They can be removed and used before they die.

The old-growth forests of the northwestern United States are home to the northern spotted owl. Harvesting the old-growth forests means death for the owls.

We want to save as many plants and animals as we can, but we also must think about what forests provide for people. We must find a balance between cutting wood for products and maintaining healthy forests. But forests cannot continue to provide us with the products we need if we don't take care of them. And we must take care of them because forests help the whole planet.

A Warmer World?

Forests help keep our climate healthy. Plants take in carbon dioxide gas (CO_2) from the air. They use it to make their food with the help of sunlight and water. After the plants have made their food, they give off oxygen. Animals breathe in this oxy-

climate = the usual weather of a region, including temperature, rainfall, and winds.

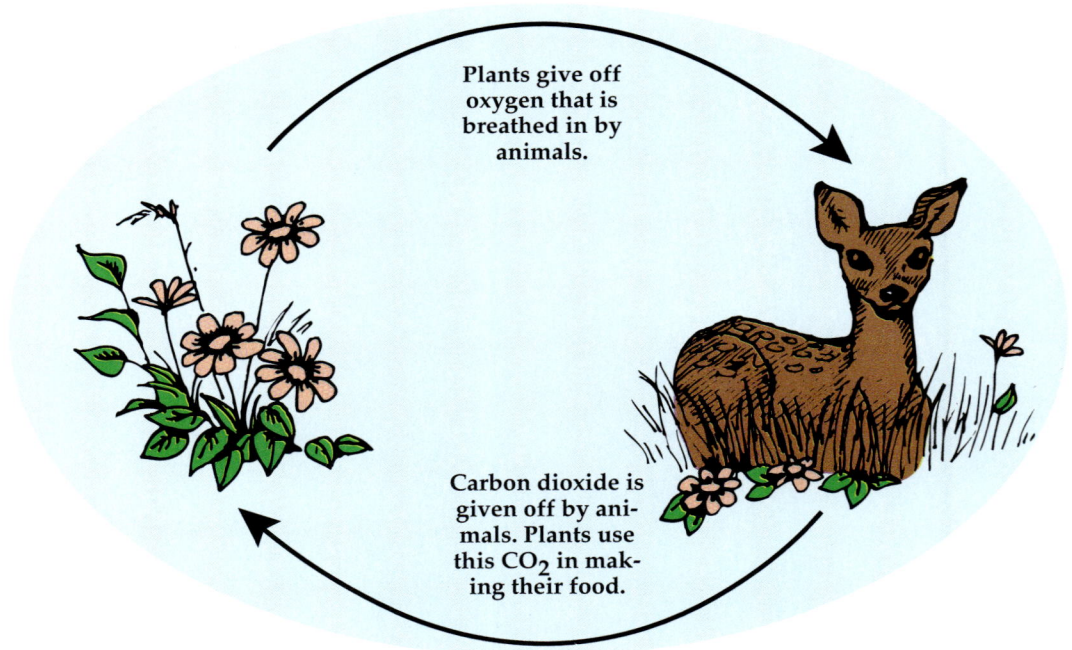

Plants give off oxygen that is breathed in by animals.

Carbon dioxide is given off by animals. Plants use this CO_2 in making their food.

gen and breath out carbon dioxide.

When there were fewer people on Earth, this exchange of gases was balanced. But then humans started building factories that burn coal and oil. We build cars and trucks for transportation that burn gasoline. Coal, oil, and gasoline give off carbon dioxide when they burn. Many scientists believe people today are putting too much carbon dioxide into the air.

Every day more carbon dioxide is released into our atmosphere. At the same time, we are cutting down forests that take carbon dioxide out of the air.

Carbon dioxide is a gas that traps the sun's heat in our atmosphere. Scientists think the planet's climate is getting warmer because more carbon dioxide is in the air, trapping the sun's heat. The more forests we cut down, the fewer trees are left to take the carbon dioxide out of the air, and the warmer the Earth's climate may get.

As the climate warms, the plants and animals we know may not be able to adjust to the new conditions. Some species may die out, others may flourish. As the ocean water gets warmer, the level of the sea could rise because warm water takes up more space than cool water. Many coastal areas would be underwater. Global warming could change the world dramatically.

Some scientists believe all the carbon dioxide we are putting into the air will make Earth warmer. This could cause the climate to change.

Being a City Forester

Forests don't have to be a great distance away. Throughout North America, people are getting together to plant trees in their cities and towns. Trees release oxygen into the air. Trees also make the cities look pretty. Many people get help from the Global ReLeaf program of American Forests or from the National Arbor Day Foundation.

In Baltimore, Maryland, 1,200 schoolchildren helped plant 6,000 trees. In 1987, the state of Maryland got money to plant trees along its streams and rivers to help keep pollution out of Chesapeake Bay. But there was a catch. All the trees had to be planted in one month. So school children in Baltimore helped out. They planted trees along riverbanks in their city. When the school children see the trees they planted, they know that they helped their city—and nature, too.

At a big celebration, the mayor made a speech. He said, "I hope you will one day walk beneath the trees you have planted here.

Maybe you will come back when you have children of your own. You can tell them 'I planted that tree when I was in school.' "

Trees planted in cities make a different kind of forest—an urban forest. But they help keep our planet from getting too warm. Not only do they absorb carbon dioxide, but they also can help save electricity by shading houses during the summer so we don't need air-conditioners. And city birds have more places to nest.

Chances are, there is a tree-planting group near you. LowCountry ReLeaf plants trees in Charleston, South Carolina (right), and Trees Atlanta works in Atlanta, Georgia (opposite). San Francisco's Friends of the Urban Forest has planted more than 7,000 trees. Farther North, Friends of Trees in Portland, Oregon, helps young people reforest their city. Philadelphia Green helps neighborhood people in that Pennsylvania city plant trees on their streets. The Twin Cities Tree Trust gives kids summer jobs planting trees around Minneapolis-St. Paul. To date, the kids have planted an amazing 300,000 trees. New York, Atlanta, and Los Angeles also have successful tree-planting programs.

Find a group in your city and join the successful foresters!

A Drier World?

Trees take in water through their roots. The water moves upward to every part of the tree—all the branches and all the leaves. After using it, the tree gives off leftover water through its leaves. The water rises into the air and into clouds. Then the water falls again as rain.

When forests are cut down, areas that once had good rainfall may get no rain at all. There are no longer trees to release water into rain clouds. In this way, the destruction of forests may cause the climate to get drier.

Walking through a forest on a beautiful day makes many people feel glad to be alive.

A Sadder World?

Finally, people need forests. We need forest products such as wood and paper. We also eat the nuts from forest trees and the berries from forest bushes.

People need forests for many other reasons. Some people love to walk through the deep, shaded silence of a forest. Forests are beautiful, even magical, places. It would be a sadder and poorer world if all our forests were cut down.

Forests are important to people, animals, and plants. No one says that people should not cut trees for wood and paper. Trees are a renewable resource and, if managed wisely, may continue to flourish. The question is, can we use our forests wisely? We need to seek out ways to harvest forest products inexpensively and responsibly without destroying the whole forest environment.

Weeds and Wonder Drugs

The yew tree grows in old, uncut forests of the northwestern United States. For many years, lumber companies and the U.S. Forest Service treated the yew tree as a weed because it has no value as lumber. After a forest was clear-cut, yew trees were burned with other "trash" plants.

Several years ago, scientists who work for drug companies began studying the yew tree. They were amazed to find that the bark of the yew contains a chemical called taxol that is helpful in treating certain kinds of cancer.

The call went out to the Forest Service and the lumber companies. Stop killing yew trees! Stop clear-cutting old-growth forests! Loggers now are supposed to leave yew trees alone when they cut the other trees.

Scientists are trying to make taxol in laboratories now, and they may have found other sources of this wonderful chemical. But if all the northwestern forests had been cut down, we might never have known about this helpful drug. There's really no such thing as a "trash" plant!

The Nature of Forests

Forests are moist places. Forest plants continually give off water, so rain is usually common and plentiful. Trees and shrubs are kings of the forest. The leafy cover makes forests dark and mysterious. The plants on the forest floor survive on the little sunlight that peeks through the leaves.

A forest is like a city of plants. The tallest trees are like skyscrapers. Smaller trees are like shorter apartment buildings. Large homes and stores are the bushes. Small buildings are like little plants on the forest floor. There is even life underground, as there is in a city with a subway system. Each level of the forest "city" contains different kinds of plants and animals. This rich mix of living things is what makes a forest. It is a complex environment in which every level provides habitats for many living things.

A healthy forest is a mixture of all kinds of plants.

habitat = the specific environment of a plant or animal, including soil, weather, landforms, and other living things.

Forest Animals

Animals of all kinds live in one or more of these forest layers. Some animals spend most of their time in the treetops. Owls swoop down on prey from their treetop perches. Flying squirrels glide through the air from branch to branch. All kinds of squirrels build their nests high in the trees. Many birds, such as warblers and redstarts, nest in treetops. Woodpeckers spend much of their lives in the

trees. They peck into the bark to find insects to eat.

Other animals scurry around on the forest floor. Ovenbirds nest and find food among the rotting leaves. Wild turkeys gobble through the undergrowth, and mice scurry through the leaves. Deer nibble the sweet leaves of bushes and small trees, while bears get fat stuffing themselves with berries. Chipmunks dart about, looking for nuts. Foxes prowl the forest hunting for small animals. Box turtles tug tasty earthworms out of the ground.

Below the Ground

As in a prairie, much of what grows above the forest floor depends on what exists beneath the ground. Under the litter of rotting leaves and fallen logs lies a whole world of living things. Billions of earthworms and insects churn and enrich the forest soil.

Have you ever walked through a forest or a tree-lined park after it rains? The earth is soft and wet. The air smells clean and sweet from the newly washed leaves, and the ground sends up the rich scent of the soil. As you walk through the forest, you may see lots of strange-looking mushrooms.

Mushrooms belong to a group of living things called fungi. The cap-shaped mushroom you see on the forest floor is just part of the fungus. The cap contains seeds called spores.

But a very important part of a fungus lies under ground. Under the soil, the main part of a living fungus looks like a fine web of silk threads. The silken webs of many fungi live on and among tree roots. Some of these fungi help the tree take in nutrients from the soil. Many trees cannot survive without certain kinds of fungi around their roots. A healthy forest needs rich soil in which fungi can live and—sometimes—help trees grow.

Not all fungi are good for trees, however. Mushrooms around the base of a tree can mean the tree is being "attacked" by fungi. These fungi are actually harmful to the tree.

Kinds of Forests

Forests are found all over the world. Evergreen forests of pine and other cone-bearing trees grow in the cold, windy environments of the north or high on mountains. Tropical rain forests grow in hot, wet places. Most of these are also evergreen.

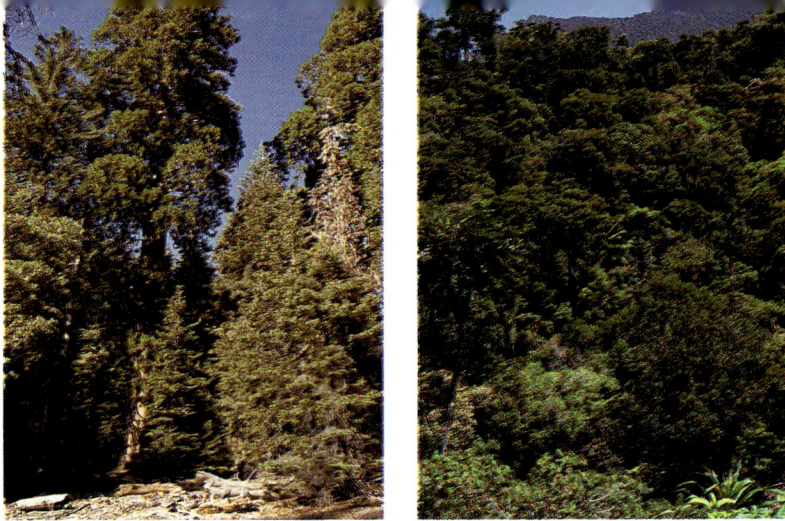

Many forests have trees whose broad leaves fall off in winter. These forests grow in regions with moderate weather. Each kind of forest has its own special kinds of plants and animals. Each forest is perfectly suited to its region's unique climate and environment.

People and Forests

Forests have always been an important source of food, shelter, and building materials. As early people spread out across Europe, they used up their forests. When Europeans came to North America, they were amazed at the huge forests they found.

Imagine you are one of the first settlers to arrive in North America. First you cut down a few trees to make a log cabin to live in. Then you remove more trees, one by one. It is very hard work, especially taking the huge tree stumps out of the ground. Plowing the ground through the thick tree roots left in the soil is also a backbreaking task. As

Most northern forests were cut down as each state was settled. Loggers found rich forestland in Michigan during the 1800s.

each field is cleared and plowed, you plant the crop seed you brought from Europe.

Throughout eastern North America, forests became farmland. But forests seemed to be endless. The settlers could not imagine such huge forests disappearing.

More settlers came and cleared forests for farms. Some of them started lumber companies. They cut down trees to sell wood to people in towns and cities.

In the 1800s, vast areas of forest on both the East and West coasts were cut down for farming. Some of these vast woodlands were bought by lumber companies that cut down entire forests and sold the wood.

Before long, people realized that the nation's forests were disappearing. Something they thought never could happen had happened.

The same kind of forest clearing is taking place in South America. It happened in Russia when the government of the former Soviet Union sent workers into the cold, northern forests of Siberia. It's happening now in China, as that country's population grows. It's happening in Africa, too, as the people cut trees for fuel.

But all over the world today, people are beginning to realize that the old forests must be protected. And they are doing what they can to restore forests wherever possible.

An area called Landmark Pines in northern Wisconsin was deforested and burned in 1911 (above). Today it has been reforested (left).

Bringing Back the Forests

The tallest trees in the world stand on the wet West Coast and nearby mountains of northern California. These are giant redwood trees—up to 300 feet (91 meters) tall and more than 100 feet (30.5 meters) around. Many of these are more than 3,000 years old.

By the time the West was settled, the nation's demand for wood was enormous. During the Gold Rush of 1849, thousands of people with dreams of wealth flocked to California. Loggers came too. They knew many people would want to buy wood.

Giant redwood trees (above) grow in Cheatham Grove, California.

64

At that time, no laws controlled how forests were cut. Whole forests of thousand-year-old trees were cut and sold. When their deep roots rotted away, there was nothing to hold the soil in place. When heavy rains came, landslides of mud poured down the treeless mountain slopes. The mud buried towns and destroyed rivers.

In 1918, people in the area formed a group called the Save the Redwoods League. They raised money to save the remaining redwood forests and to plant redwoods on clear-cut land. Finally, in 1968, the U.S. government took steps to save some of our magnificent redwood forests. Redwood National Park in northern California was created.

Children in Kansas join in the fight to protect forests as they demonstrate to save the redwoods.

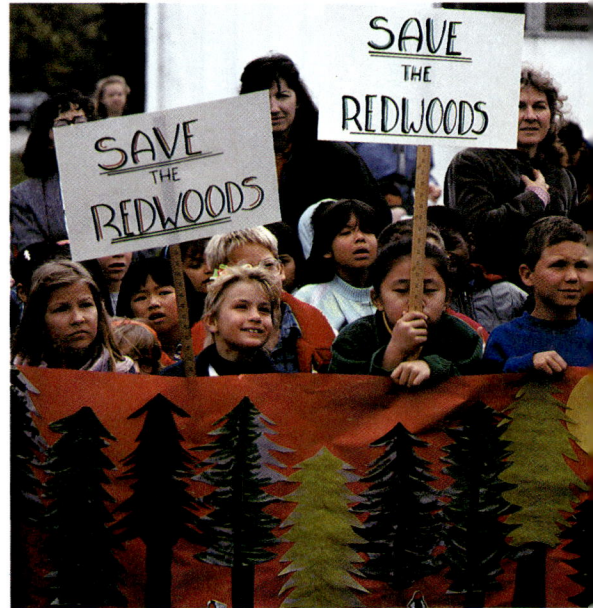

Never Again!

In 1924, six-year-old Tony Look moved with his family to the tiny town of Garberville in northern California. While his parents worked in their restaurant and raised flowers, Tony wandered the nearby redwood forests. He fell in love with the giant trees.

But soon lumber companies descended on the area. They began what they called "jack-rabbit" logging. They jumped in, clear-cut all the trees, then jumped out. Pretty soon, all the trees were gone. The results of jack-rabbit logging were devastating.

Tony Look planted a young redwood tree in Humboldt Redwoods State Park, California, in 1973.

People in northern California will never forget the great storm of 1955. In only 24 hours, 11 inches (28 centimeters) of rain fell. The mountain slopes no longer had trees to soak up the rain and hold the soil. Millions of tons of mud and gravel poured into the rivers, causing them to flood. The entire town of Garberville was buried beneath the mud.

Tony Look was sad and angry. He promised that he would do all he could to make sure this never happened again. Tony worked with the Sierra Club and the Save the Redwoods League to restore the redwood forests. Tony knew that he would not live long enough to see the restored forest, but he had to make a start.

Tony Look and other volunteers reshaped old logging roads. When it rained, these roads became canals for water and muddy soil to run down the slopes and slide off the mountain. By reshaping the roads to fit the slope of the mountain, the volunteers made the soil stay in place.

Then they planted redwood seedlings and watered them thoroughly every three weeks for two summers. Today, more than 10,000 of these young redwoods are on their thousand-year-long life journey.

seedling = a newly sprouted plant, especially a tree.

"Ever-Living" Forests

In the past on spring weekends, it was not unusual to see whole families working in cut-over redwood forests in northern California. Mothers, fathers, and children turned and raked soil. They dug holes in the ground. They planted very young trees, or seedlings, in the holes and watered them. Everyone was volunteering to help a group led by Tony Look. The group is called the Sempervirens Fund. Sempervirens, the scientific name for the giant redwoods, means "ever-living."

The Sempervirens volunteers have replanted about 300 acres (121 hectares) of redwoods in Big Basin Redwoods State Park. They have raised money to add thousands of acres of untouched redwood forest to the park. The funding comes from companies and individuals concerned about the environment. Today Sempervirens volunteers raise thousands of dollars every year by selling "gift" trees. People can pay Sempervirens to plant a tree for them or for someone they love. It is a gift that lasts a thousand years—and helps restore redwood forests.

From Old-Growth to New-Growth?

Mount St. Helens blew its top in May 1980. When the volcano that everyone thought was dead erupted, thousands of acres of trees were flattened like matchsticks. The area was lifeless, coated with gray ash.

President Jimmy Carter went to see what had happened. As his plane flew over Washington state, the president was horrified at the scene below him. He saw nothing but endless miles of bare, lifeless hills. He expressed shock that one volcano could do so much damage. A Washington state government official was embarrassed. He explained to the president that this landscape was not the work of a volcano. The devastated land that shocked the president was a clear-cut, old-growth forest.

Many foresters and other people want to see forestlands restored. Yet forests are used in so many different ways. People have just as many different ideas about how to restore, or regrow, them.

Tree Farms

Most lumber companies don't want empty land any more than the public does. They need more trees growing so that future generations will have the wood they need. Our lives would be very different without wood. But the lumber companies really don't want forests. They just want the trees.

After they clear-cut a forest, lumber companies plant trees that will produce wood they know they can sell. They plant tiny trees called seedlings. All the seedlings are of the same kind. In the Northwest, the seedlings are usually Douglas fir. Years later the companies cut and sell these trees as lumber.

Forestry workers check the growth of young tree seedlings.

The lumber companies call this process "reforestation," but it is not a forest they're restoring. An area where only one kind of tree is planted is called a tree farm. It does not have the different kinds of plants a forest has. It won't attract many kinds of wildlife. It has only one kind of wood that is good to sell.

Lumber companies usually plant trees after they have logged an area (above).

Giving Seedlings a Chance

Many scientists and foresters know that tree farms are not the answer to restoring forests. They still plant trees for lumber companies to cut, but they also grow other plants so that wildlife can live among regrown trees.

Foresters restoring clear-cuts have found ways to improve the soil. Some foresters put helpful fungi into the roots of tree seedlings before they are planted. This gives them a better chance to grow.

Other foresters prefer a more natural approach. First they plant alder bushes on clear-cut land. Alders grow quickly, and their roots and fallen leaves enrich the soil. Their roots also hold the soil in place. Alder bushes help fungi live in the soil. It is true that alders may prevent trees from growing back right away. But after 50 years or so, the alders die, leaving behind rich soil full of helpful fungi. Many foresters believe that alder is the natural healer of land damaged by clear-cutting. Some are trying to plant alder and Douglas fir together.

Sadly, lumber companies hate to wait 50 years for alders to die. Yet, the tree-farm seedlings they plant directly on burned, clear-cut land often die due to poor soil. If the companies waited, the land would be ready to grow strong, healthy trees. Having some patience may pay off for the lumber companies.

Can Nature Heal Itself?

Some foresters and scientists prefer to let nature, not people, restore clear-cut forests. Not all forests are destroyed by clear-cutting. Instead, certain kinds of forests are able to recover on their own over many years. Some forests actually may need regular cutting or burning in order to grow the same kinds of trees. However, most forests cannot recover from clear-cutting. Another way of harvesting, such as selective-cutting, should be chosen for these types of forests.

Fire used to be a natural occurrence in forest areas. Fire reduces litter buildup on the forest floor. By eliminating fire completely, branches and other litter accumulate—resulting in an even greater fire danger. Periodic cutting or burning maintains forest health and prevents large-scale forests fires in some areas of the West.

After a big fire in Yellowstone National Park, the trees and shrubs began to regrow very quickly.

Jobs and the Environment

Some towns in the Northwest rely on logging for their survival. Many workers in these towns cut down trees for lumber companies. People in these areas are afraid they will have no work if forests can't be clear-cut. However, saving forests may save—or even create—jobs.

Forests are being cleared so quickly that in 10 to 15 years there may be no forests left to cut down. Then the loggers surely will have no jobs.

But loggers could have other jobs. Lumber companies could open mills where workers cut wood into boards. The companies could pay loggers to collect seed cones or plant trees on clear-cuts. Perhaps lumber companies could go into the recycling business. Loggers could make new products out of recycled paper and wood.

Saving our old-growth forests need not cause unemployment. We can keep our ancient forests and loggers can have good jobs too.

This worker is gathering cones that will provide seeds for future trees.

Why Fish Need Trees

Loggers in the Northwest are worried about losing jobs if clear-cutting is stopped. However, clear-cutting has already cost the jobs of over 20,000 fishermen who have no work because logging has destroyed fish streams.

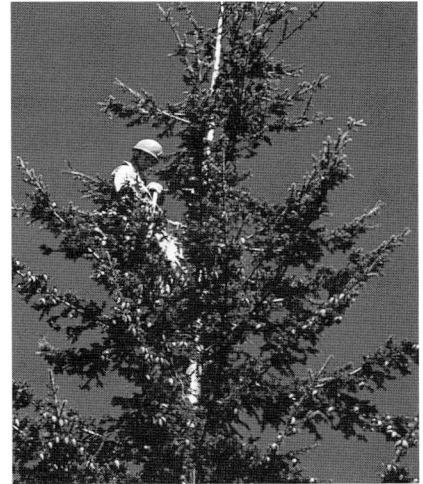

For example, lumber companies in Idaho made $14 million clear-cutting old-growth forests around the Salmon River. The logging damaged the river and destroyed nearly all the salmon. So the salmon fishermen lost $100 million.

Salmon develop from eggs laid in streams and rivers. Then they swim out of the rivers to the ocean where they live and grow. After several years, the adult salmon swim back to the same rivers where they were born. Here they mate and lay eggs. The next generation of salmon is born. Salmon need clear, shallow streams in which to lay their eggs. They need cool water shaded by trees.

In the Northwest, more than half the original salmon streams have been destroyed by clear-cutting. Clear-cutting has removed the trees along the riverbanks. Rivers are no longer shaded and cool. Mud slides have clogged the rivers where salmon laid their eggs. River water is muddy, not clear. As a result, more than 200 kinds of salmon and other fish are disappearing from many rivers.

This man is replanting trees on a slope along the bank of the Mattole River.

Forests for Fuel

In North America, most forests are cut to make paper or wood products such as furniture. In other parts of the world, however, forests often are cut by poor people who live near them. These people use the wood to burn as fuel for cooking and heat.

Mad About the Mattole

The Mattole River salmon were among the last in the Northwest to swim freely upriver as they have for thousands of years. But by 1970, most of the forest around the Mattole River in northern California was clear-cut. When it rained, mud slid down the bare mountain slopes into the river. The salmon could no longer lay their eggs in the river. The salmon were in danger of dying out.

People who live around the Mattole River decided to save their river and the salmon. They attacked the problem in several ways. Volunteers planted trees and smaller plants on the clear-cut slopes to hold the soil in place. That helped stop mud slides.

The people built hatch boxes for the salmon. They put boxes containing clean gravel in the river. The boxes had filters that kept out soil and mud. Then the volunteers got live adult salmon. After the salmon mated, the people put the eggs in the hatch boxes. Most eggs hatched. The baby salmon grew until they swam out to the ocean.

Now the people of the Mattole River are watching the river and the lumber companies. They are making sure that logging no longer will cause mud to foul the river. They are helping keep the river clear. The annual salmon runs that were almost a thing of the past are getting better. Salmon are returning to small streams where they hadn't laid eggs for years. The people who volunteered to help the Mattole and its salmon hope that restoring the forest and the river will keep the salmon coming back.

SUCCESS STORY

In many of these countries, the number of people is increasing rapidly. More and more people need more and more wood. Vast areas of forest have been cut for fuel. For years, neither the people nor their governments replanted any trees. The bare soil was blowing away. Land that once was covered with forests was becoming empty desert.

The country of Kenya in East Africa has much land that is turning to desert because the trees are gone. Wangari Maathai is a Kenyan woman with a goal. In 1977, she started the Green Belt Movement of Kenya to help restore forests. Many Kenyan people have joined the movement. They plant trees to hold the soil in place and to cut for fuel. Some Kenyan women work in tree nurseries where seedlings are grown. The Green Belt workers of Kenya have planted more than 20 million trees. The desert is being pushed back.

Wangari Maathai
(left in the photo)
started the Green
Belt Movement of
Kenya. Her move-
ment is spreading
to other African
nations.

The Tree Hugger

One day in India, an old man named Bahuguna decided that what kept the people poor was a ruined environment. He realized that the loss of forests left the people with nothing. He understood that cutting trees causes landslides and ruins the soil. So he decided to do something to help his people. Bahuguna began the Chipko movement. The word *chipko* means "hug," as in "hug a tree."

Bahuguna visits villages all over India. He speaks gently to the children and adults in the villages. Sometimes he teaches them a song about a talking tree. The tree says, "Do not touch me with an ax. I, too, feel pain. I am your friend. I bring you fresh air. I bring you water. I always bow down before you. Why do you cut me down?"

Thousands of poor people, especially women and children, work with Chipko. Many of them go out together and hug trees. This stops loggers from cutting these trees down.

The Chipko people also plant trees where forests used to be. They plant trees that will grow quickly. In a few years, they can be cut for fuel. Then older trees won't have to be cut. Chipko teaches that if you cut a tree, you must plant another tree in its place. In this way, Chipko is protecting forests and providing fuelwood for people, too.

Dear Mr. Preisdent   Aug. 4, 1989
Please, will you do somthing about pollution. I want to keep on living till I am 100 years old WRITE now I am 9 years old. My name is Melissa. You and other people maybe you could put up signs SAYING: STOP POLLUTION ITS KILLING the world. PLEASE Help me. STOP pollution. Mr. Preisdent Please if you ecnor this letter soon we will die of pollution of the ozon layer. PLease Help

Saving Forests

Nine-year-old Melissa Poe of Nashville, Tennessee, sent this letter to President Bush in 1989. She never got a reply. So Melissa got in touch with an advertising company that creates ads to help the environment. The ad company put Melissa's letter on 250 huge signs around the United States. It even put one up in Washington, D.C., where the president lives. They put up the signs for free.

Melissa was so encouraged by this that she started a group in her school. She called it Kids For A Clean Environment, or Kids' FACE. Melissa's friends and classmates wrote letters to Congress.

They worked to clean up their local environment, and they planted trees around their state. In time, Kids' FACE had more than 110,000 members all over North America.

Kids' FACE is working with the Children's Alliance for the Protection of the Environment, or CAPE. Both groups are helping the U.S. Forest Service and the U.S. Fish and Wildlife Service to preserve native forests in the United States.

They began by creating a marked trail especially for kids in Yellowstone National Park in Wyoming. The trail through the forest was a great success. The children wished kids everywhere could experience their own native forests. Kids' FACE and CAPE are trying to help create many Children's Forests.

Melissa Poe presented $5,000 for the establishment of Children's Fire Trail in Yellowstone National Park. The trail winds through new regrowth in a burned forest. Children learn that fire is part of a healthy forest.

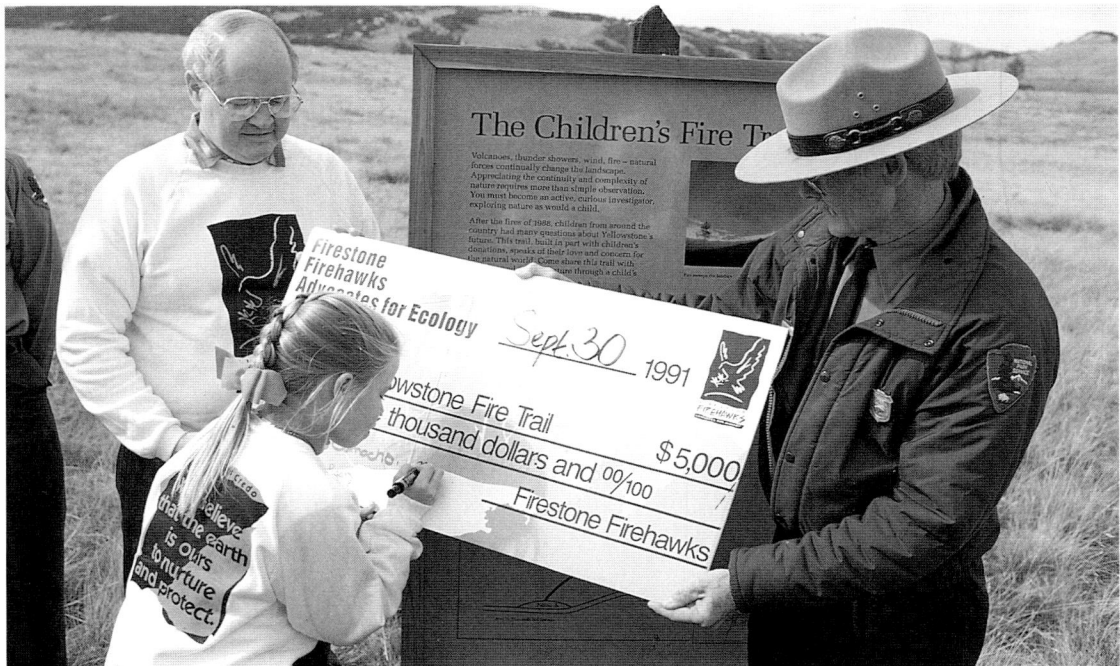

The children hope that Children's Forests will one day exist in parts of all our national forests or wildlife refuges. Trees will not be cut there. Many animals will live in the forests the children are trying to preserve.

In the Halls of Power

The students from a school in West Chester, Pennsylvania, wrote letters to the editor of their local newspaper. People were impressed. The National Wildlife Federation decided to help the students travel to Oregon to speak before a government committee deciding the fate of the northern spotted owl. The students argued for protection of old-growth forests to save the owl.

These students are really interested in helping the environment. They even went to Washington, D.C., to talk with members of Congress. The students in this picture are urging a congressman to vote in favor of forests. They explained their point of view. They asked the Congresspeople to vote for laws to save old-growth forests and other threatened environments.

These students made their voices heard in the "halls of power" in Washington. They learned that all people can help the environment by letting lawmakers know how they feel about environmental problems.

Working for Change

Many people want to preserve what is left of North America's ancient, uncut forests. Some members of Congress have introduced laws that would protect America's remaining old-growth forests forever. But lumber companies and some congressional members from the Northwest do not want these laws. Both groups need to work together with people concerned about the environment to ensure the survival of all the different types of forests and their wildlife.

The public, environmental groups, and groups such as Kids' FACE are asking lawmakers to protect the remaining old-growth forests. They know that once such forests are destroyed, it may take hundreds of years for them to be restored. And plants and animals of the forest may become extinct if the forests are not protected now.

These children in Wisconsin are learning about forests through an environmental education program. They are hugging an old-growth white pine tree.

Clear-Cut Canada

The Western Canada Wilderness Committee was formed in 1987 with 500 members. Today, it has more than 25,000 members. Hundreds, sometimes thousands, of these people protest forest clear-cutting. The magnificent ancient forests of British Columbia, on Canada's West Coast, are being destroyed. If things don't change, all the forests will be gone within 15 years. The forests are being clear-cut at a rate of 600,000 acres (243,000 hectares) every year.

British Columbia earns lots of money from tourists. The province calls itself "Super, Natural" to attract tourists, but untouched nature is found in only a few national parks.

Vancouver Island's Kyuquot people are trying to save their native land. For thousands of years they hunted elk and fished for salmon. Today, clear-cutting threatens to destroy their way of life on the Tahsish River. The Kyuquot chief says, "The Tahsish is where we hunt for elk. It is where we get fish. It is the only good river left. All the others are brown and dirty."

Many people in British Columbia want the world to know what is happening to their forests. They have made videos that show the destruction

This old-growth rain forest in British Columbia is scheduled for logging. The Western Canada Wilderness Committee has been building a trail in the area so people can see its beauty and join the fight to save it.

of their forests, and they hope tourists will stay away until the clear-cutting is stopped.

Alberta and the Athabasca

A group of lumber companies in Alberta, Canada, made a deal with the government. With the help of millions of government dollars, the companies would be allowed to clear-cut 77,000 square miles (200,000 square kilometers) of Alberta forests. That's about the size of the state of Nebraska.

The lumber companies planned to cut down many aspen trees. When made into paper, an aspen tree is worth $100. As wood, it is worth $50. Yet the Canadian government is selling Alberta's

Aspen forests in Alberta are in danger of being cut for paper.

aspen trees to lumber companies for less than $1 each. In this case, it seems that destroying the environment really pays.

The government never had studied the environmental effects of its plan. But citizens know that their environment will be hurt by this project. William Fuller and other Albertans started a group called Friends of the Athabasca. The Athabasca River and the Peace River will be polluted by paper mills. The fish will be poisoned, the animals that eat the fish will be poisoned, and the people who eat the fish will be poisoned.

Friends of the Athabasca, scientists, and others have stopped the project—for a while. The government has agreed to study the effect of the plan on the environment. Albertans hope the government realizes it's a bad plan. They are working to make sure that Alberta is not clear-cut and polluted.

Fishing and recreation in Alberta's Athabasca River region can be seriously damaged by paper mills.

Saving Siberia

Siberia is a huge region that extends from central Russia to the Pacific Ocean. The evergreen forests of Siberia, called taiga, cover an area as large as the entire United States.

The climate in Siberia is harsh and cold. Trees grow slowly. Siberian tigers, elk, foxes, ermine, and birds struggle to survive. The taiga region is so fragile that if it is disturbed, it will never recover.

In Russia today, the people and the government are in great need of money. Some Russians want to clear-cut the Siberian forests and sell the wood. Other people want to preserve the forests for their wildlife and their future.

Some local officials in Siberia have allowed lumber companies from the United States, Japan, and South Korea to clear-cut, even though it is against the law. Russian environment officials and forest scientists are fighting the clear-cutting. So are native Siberian people. The native Khant people, for example, herd reindeer. Reindeer eat plants in and near the forests. Without the forests, the reindeer—and the Khant people—will be ruined.

Siberian evergreen forest, called taiga, consists of many trees and few shrubs or smaller trees.

The Rain Forest Crunch

Have you ever eaten Rain Forest Crunch candy or Ben and Jerry's Rainforest Crunch ice cream? Have you eaten Rain Forest Crisp cereal for breakfast? If your answer is yes, you have helped native people save their rain-forest home.

Tropical rain forests are wet forests filled with countless kinds of plants and animals. They are found in 80 countries that lie near the equator. They

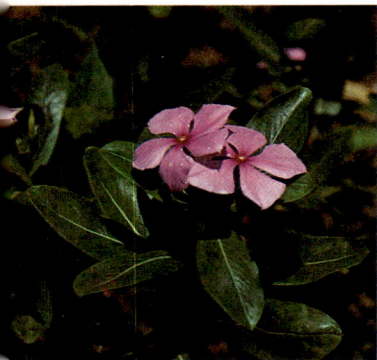

The rosy periwinkle is used to make medicine for treating certain kinds of cancer.

The mantled howler monkey lives in the rain forests of Costa Rica in Central America.

circle our planet like an enormous green belt. Because rain forests contain such a large number of trees and plants, they help control the world climate. These huge forests are called "the lungs of the Earth" because they take in tons of carbon dioxide and give off tons of oxygen into the air.

Rain forests have more different species of living things than any other environment on Earth. While a North American forest might have a dozen kinds of trees in one acre (0.4 hectare), a rain forest has hundreds.

Some rain-forest plants, such as the rosy periwinkle, are used to treat diseases such as cancer. Scientists agree that rain forests have thousands of plants we haven't even identified yet. Some of them may contain useful medicines that we will lose if rain forests are destroyed.

Rain forests are home to more animal species than any other environment. Nobody knows just

how many there are. Scientists studying insects in a rain forest found that a single tree was home to more than 100 different insect species. Scientists never had seen many of these insects before. If loggers keep cutting rain forests, how many wonderful animals and plants may disappear before we even know they exist?

The world's tropical rain forests are shown in the dark areas on the map. Railroad ties are made from strong rain-forest wood (below).

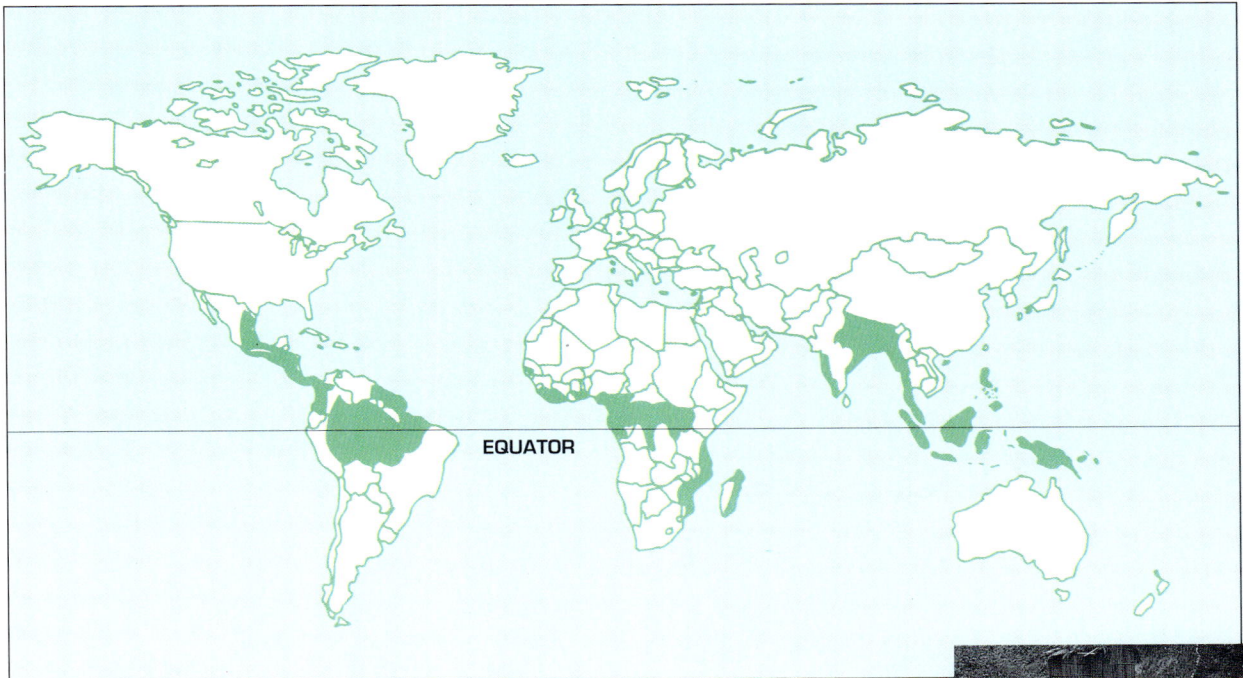

EQUATOR

Gone Forever

Unfortunately, rain forests are not like most of the forests in North America. Once they are cut down they cannot be restored.

Rain forests look so lush and green and rich that it is hard to believe the soil under them is very thin and poor in nutrients. So many plants grow

there that they take almost all the nutrients out of the soil. In a rain forest, nutrients are found in the plants, rather than the soil. So when a rain forest is clear-cut and burned, all the nutrients are burned and become ash. The ash only can support crops for two to three years. After clear-cutting and burning, some kinds of rain-forest soil may change into a kind of rock-hard cement.

For all these reasons, it is important that people preserve what we can of the rain forests instead of trying to restore them.

The web of life in rain forests has been evolving for millions of years. Unfortunately, all it takes is a few hours of cutting and burning to destroy this delicate environment.

Burning the Land

For centuries, many native peoples have grown crops in the rain forest. Some, such as the Mentawi Islanders of Indonesia, do not burn the forest at all before they plant their crops. They simply plant their seeds among the trees and plants of the rain forest.

Today, however, the government of Brazil has encouraged many poor people to move out of the cities and into the Amazon rain forest. Many settlers clear forestland to grow crops or graze cattle. They use a primitive method of clearing land called slash-and-burn. These settlers cut down, or slash, huge areas of rain forest. Then they burn the cut material. So many settlers burn so much that the Amazon fires can be seen from outer space.

For a year or two, crops or grasses grow well on the cleared land. Then weeds start taking over. So ranchers burn the land again and again. Finally, no plants are left to rot and enrich the soil. Soon the soil is ruined forever. The farmers and ranchers then move somewhere else.

Lumber companies that clear-cut rain forests also set fires. Like loggers in North America, after clear-cutting they burn all the leftover logs and "weeds" on the ground. The soil of the rain forest is destroyed. Rain-forest areas cleared and burned in this way may never recover. Areas of rain forest in Cambodia that were cleared more than 600 years ago still have not recovered.

Rain-forest land cleared using the slash-and-burn method will not support crops for very long. It will be abandoned.

Protest in Ecuador

It was a remarkable sight. Ten thousand people were gathered in the streets of Quito, the capital of Ecuador. Some wore bright feathers. Some wore colorful native clothing. Others carried spears. Native people had come to ask the government of Ecuador to save their homes. Some had walked 300 miles (483 kilometers) to join this protest that was held in April 1992.

Native lands in the Amazon rain forest were being ruined by logging and oil drilling. The native people wanted the government of Ecuador to protect the rain forest.

Since the early 1970s, more than 12 million acres (4.9 million hectares) of Amazon rain forest

The Shuar people live in the rain forest of eastern Ecuador. Their way of life is threatened when the forest is cut.

have been given to oil companies. Millions of gallons of oil and other poisons have spilled or been dumped in the forest. Fish and wild animals can no longer live there. The people are being poisoned too.

The government of Ecuador agreed to give native people one-half of their homeland. The oil companies could keep the other half. The people were not satisfied.

When an oil spill poisoned the Napo River in August 1992, the Ecuadorean natives protested again. They joined forces with environmental groups from all over South America to ask that all their land be returned to them. Environmental groups continue to support the Ecuadorean people in their fight.

Drilling for oil is big business in the upper Amazon jungle of Ecuador in South America.

A Matter of Money

Every minute of every day, about 80 acres (32 hectares) of the world's rain forests are clear-cut. As a result, about 48 species of living things become extinct every day.

Many rain forests are found in poor countries that owe money to banks around the world. These countries cut their rain forests and sell the wood to pay back their loans. But this makes no sense. These countries sell one acre (0.4 hectare) of clear-cut lumber for $1,000, but they could make $6,800 by gathering other products from one acre of healthy, preserved rain forest.

Some products that come from rain forests without harming them include:

• Rain Forest Crunch and other products made with cashew nuts, Brazil nuts, and coconut.

• Products made with fruits gathered from healthy rain forests. These include papaya and pineapple.

• Products made with tropical honey.

• Buttons made from Tagua nuts.

• Soaps, perfumes, and oils made out of rain-forest plants.

Protect by Recycling

Forests all over the world need to be protected so that the entire planet can be healthy. We can help save our forests by recycling as much paper

recycling = the process of collecting used, scrap, or waste material and making it into new products. This is the symbol for recycling.

as possible. Newspapers, junk mail, school paper, computer paper, packaging, and cardboard can all be recycled and made into new paper products. You can help by buying recycled notebook paper and home paper products. You also can use fewer paper products and less wood. Above all, avoid buying precious rain-forest woods such as teak and mahogany.

Connecting with Nature

It is within our power to rebuild prairies and forests, but people never can do as good a job—or be as patient—as nature. What people can rebuild is only a shadow of the original.

Every part of our environment is in trouble today—rivers, forests, deserts, prairies, plants, animals, air, and the land itself. The more natural treasures we protect today, the less we will need to restore tomorrow.

Both prairies, such as the Chippewa Prairie in Minnesota (above), and forests, such as the Manú National Park rain forest in Peru (below), need to be preserved.

Children and the Rain Forest

Roland Riensuu, a young student in Sweden, became very concerned about the destruction of rain forests. He started the Children's Rain Forest in an effort to save them. Children from all over the world raise money to send to the Children's Rain Forest or other groups, such as the Rainforest Action Network. The Children's Rain Forest uses the money to buy acres of rain forest so that they can never be cut.

Children raise money in many ways. For example, children in New York State sold toys, books, and puzzles. A San Francisco boy raised $500 with a rainforest read-a-thon. Students in a Virginia school raised money by having a walk-a-thon for the rain forest. Bake sales, concerts, films, parties, washing cars, bike-a-thons—you name it. There are many ways to raise money to preserve a few acres of rain forest. The few acres add up—almost 20,000 acres (8,000 hectares) of rain forest in Costa Rica (above) are protected now as a result of young Roland's interest.

PLACES TO WRITE

You can get more information or find out what you can do to help by writing to one of these organizations:

American Forests
1516 P St., NW
Washington, DC 20005

CAPE
P.O. Box 307
Austin, TX 78767

Children's Rain Forest
P.O. Box 936
Lewiston, ME 04240

Kids' FACE
P.O. Box 158254
Nashville, TN 37215

Kids for Saving Earth
P.O. Box 47247
Plymouth, MN 55447

Kids Network
National Geographic Society
Educational Services Dept., 1001
Washington, DC 20077

Kids Save the Planet
P.O. Box 471
Forest Hills, NY 11375

The Land Institute
2440 E. Water Well Rd.
Salina, KS 67401

Missouri Prairie Foundation
P.O. Box 200
Columbia, MO 65205

National Arbor Day Foundation
100 Arbor Ave.
Nebraska City, NE 68410

The Nature Conservancy
1815 N. Lynn St.
Arlington, VA 22209

Rainforest Action Network (RAN)
450 Sansome, Suite 700
San Francisco, CA 94111

Save the Redwoods League
114 Sansome St., Rm 605
San Francisco, CA 94104

YES! (Youth for Environmental Sanity)
706 Frederick St.
Santa Cruz, CA 95062

GLOSSARY

aquifer – an underground area of rock and sand that collects water that seeps through the soil after rain.

clear-cut – stripped bare of all trees, bushes, and other growth. Clear-cut land is usually burned after it is cut.

climate – the usual weather of a region, including temperature, rainfall, and winds.

crossbreed – to grow new plants that combine the characteristics of two different species.

drought – a period of little or no rainfall.

endangered – in danger of dying out completely; almost extinct.

enrich – to add nutrients.

extinct – no longer in existence.

fertile – very rich and able to support life.

fungi – a group of plantlike living things that must obtain their food from other living things. Includes mushrooms, molds, and yeasts. A single fungi is called a **fungus**.

habitat – the specific environment of a plant or animal, including soil, weather, landforms, and other living things.

nutrients – the chemical substances plants and animals need to live and grow.

old-growth forest – forest that has never been cut.

recycling – the process of collecting used, scrap, or waste material and making it into new products.

restore – to return to the original condition.

savanna – a tropical or subtropical grassland with coarse grasses and a few scattered trees.

selective cutting – cutting some trees while leaving others standing, as opposed to clear-cutting.

seedling – a newly sprouted plant, especially a tree.

sod – prairie soil held together in a solid mat by grass roots.

species – one kind of plant or animal. Usually members of a species mate only with each other.

steppe – open, dry, flat land with short grasses, especially the plains of Russia and Ukraine.

urban forest – trees growing in urban areas.

INDEX

ABOUT THE AUTHOR

Natalie Goldstein is a freelance writer specializing in the environment, life sciences, and education. She holds a Master's Degree in Environmental Science/Communications from SUNY Syracuse, and a Master's Degree in Education from CUNY City College (Permanent NYS Teacher's Certification).